Praise for *A Stranger In my Skin*

✠

"The voice of the Spirit makes itself heard in time and circumstances prompted by the healing energy of Wisdom. In our world this "voicing" calls for a concrete vehicle of expression. Sister Jill's life, spoken in vigorous honesty and openness, comes at a time of great struggle and unrest for us all. Here, in this life-story, we experience a fierce courage, a sensitive, listening and obedient heart and mind answering life's promptings with extraordinary imagination, talent, and humility.

This book should be in the hands of young and old, hungry for the peace and serenity born of realistic optimism. In this, Sister Jill's work offers us a precious gift of sacred proportions."

—Thomas A. Francoeur, M.A. EdD.
Professor/Psychologist, McGill University.

"For many years I have been inspired by Sr. Jill Aigner, O.S.B., by her beautiful (audio-visual) contemplative prayer series, used often in my retreat ministry; by her amazing faith and courage in co-founding, funding and rescuing the beautifully-situated Bethlehem Retreat Center in Nanaimo, BC on Vancouver Island, Canada; and by her life-long efforts to encourage, teach and empower others, especially women, towards service and leadership in our church and in our world.

Her autobiography moved me to tears. It will move others, especially victims of childhood trauma, to reach for the stars and gratefully embrace their call to a healing union with our loving God."

—Fr. Armand M. Nigro, S.J.

A Stranger In My Skin

National Library of Canada Cataloguing In Publication

Aigner, Jill, 1923-
A stranger in my skin : an unconventional path to God / Jill Aigner.

ISBN 978-0-9735277-2-8

1. Aigner, Jill, 1923-.
2. House of Bread Monastery (Nanaimo, B.C.)—Biography.
3. Benedictines—British Columbia—Nanaimo—Biography.

I. Title.

BX4705.A34A4 2007   271'.97   C2007-900694-9

Cover Photo: *Shrine at Matterhorn* by Sister Jill Aigner
Editing by Hiro Boga
Cover & text design by Hiro Boga
Printed in Canada by Hignell Book Printing on recycled paper

Published by Monastery Press
2329 Arbot Rd
Nanaimo, BC
V9R 6S8
Canada
www.houseofbreadmonastery.com

✠

A Stranger
In My Skin

An Unconventional Path to God

✠

a memoir

by Sister Jill Aigner, OSB

Monastery Press
2007

✠

I dedicate this book to all those who have accompanied me through my long life. My grandmothers, parents, siblings, husband and children have all placed their imprint on my life. My Benedictine Sisters here at House of Bread Monastery and in Mt. Angel have encouraged my vocation and supported me during my thirty-five years in religious life; sometimes not easy for them, nor for me, for my religious life is a very unconventional journey. Retreatants and friends have encouraged me to share my life story.

A word here, a glance there, a sign of awareness, a spark in response to an interaction—even people I knew slightly or not at all have given me significant support, or helped me go in another direction, or opened a new door that had to be investigated.

The God presence in each person has opened me to a deeper personal interaction with my God. In particular, I thank Sister Eileen and my Spiritual Director who has guided me these last years.

I have told my story in the hope that it will help others realize how common are the woes and joys presented to us in our lifetime. Sometimes it has been a help to know that others, in or out of religious life, have experienced similar tribulations, have somehow resolved them and gone on to a fuller and more fruitful life.

✠

There are two voices that speak in this book. One is a casual voice, a chronological telling of my story. The second voice, a reflective one, is drawn from my reflections and the journals I have kept since the turn of the century. A much damaged child, I struggled all my life to break the spell of my early years. My journaling voice speaks of how God helped me to recognize, understand, and accept the skewed life I have led and to integrate all my life, embracing the shadow and painful, varied events. My growth did not take place according to any pattern, but unfolded through an openness and willingness to look at any shadow that presented itself; reflect on each dark portion, work it free, reconcile myself to it, and continue on my passage to light and the fullness of life. It is my hope that by telling the story of my own journey, others may realize the importance of understanding, deep in their heart, the wondrous continuing call of God to a life that recognizes the unconditional loving, nurturing presence of God.

✠

PILGRIM JOURNEY

I am a pilgrim, solitary, alone, yet never closer
to my Creator
I walk an unknown path
my vision clear, ears open, senses sharpened
listen quietly to hear the call

My life is simple
my journey revealed as I discern signs   directions
many paths before me, crossing the paths of   others
distance difficult to measure, progress unclear

I encounter dangers, natural barriers, people
share my gifts, sometimes my fears
I come to a resting place, protected from storms of my
  own making,
barrenness, death from which new life springs.

The evening hour, stillness, calls me to reflection
to a depth of presence
I am not afraid to walk into darkness
silence speaks and comforts me.

I cross valleys, climb mountains, go down into the
  desert
walk along the ocean shore, in the depth of the forest
into the darkness of soul
where only my Creator   is heard

I am watered and fed by my Creator
the whole length of the path
a pilgrim on life's journey

TABLE OF CONTENTS

MESSAGE FROM GOD

In late June 2002, while driving from Duncan, British Columbia toward Nanaimo, I felt compelled to change direction. I was driving home alone from a funeral. I had been thinking of my Aunt Hilda; her imminent death at 101 would leave me as the eldest in our family. The ministry at the Bethlehem Retreat Center, of which I was Director, had received a near death blow. The Diocese of Victoria was in a financial crisis that forced them to put the Retreat Centre up for sale. Our Benedictine House of Bread Monastery had to buy the property or go out of business. We were in the midst of a fund-raising drive to make the final purchase. I was thinking of these things as I drove along. Suddenly, I felt unsafe—a very unusual feeling for me; the feeling was so sharp it demanded my full attention. As I approached Lakes Road, I knew I must go to the Poor

Clares Monastery and ask to speak to one of the Sisters. Right then I knew I did not have a choice. It was imperative that I say out loud, to someone, that I felt unsafe to continue driving, otherwise I could be in grave trouble. My body was shaking and I felt cold.

This was a very strong, compelling message from God. I made the correct turns, stopped, rang the doorbell, and asked for the Sister. I had met her a few times over the years but in no sense knew her. She came into the parlour, and as we met I blurted out, "I don't feel safe". Somehow I trusted she would hear beyond the few words I could get out. I am sure she noticed my shaking, my quaking voice. We shared a bit and she gently asked me, "Are you lonely?" My answer was an immediate "Yes. I am." My answer surprised me. How could I be lonely living in a religious community and being fully involved in ministry? "How can I help?" she asked. " I'm not sure; I'm not sure what would help; I am not good at voicing my personal needs. It's like I'm partially caught in a web and I realize I can't share my dilemma."

It became obvious to me that I could not untangle myself, become free, without help. We talked for about twenty minutes or so, and then I felt better and left. She invited me to come back if I chose. In reviewing my journals, I found in late May, 2001, perhaps my first voicing of the predicament that made me stop in Duncan in late June of 2002.

May 31, 2001. I need, according to a friend, to not put on a mask or blinders, but to find something soft to put around me to protect me. I need something that will bring in light and truth, a shield that will warm me and not be a hard object, as it was once. The thing that comes to mind is a spider web, so beautiful on frosty mornings. They are gossamer thin, yet are tough, in that they can take on early morning dew, then during the middle of the day they take on their dry stance and last for days.

Lord, give me a web with many strengthening points to protect me from harsh blasts of others. I need to take reflective time, let the messages in, trap them as a spider does, then allow them to die without ever touching me.

Today I realize that I no longer feel unsafe and trapped. With God's help, the web is now a protection and safe shelter for me. This was a forerunner of the kind of transformation God wanted within me. My musings of late have made me more aware of the true depth of my life story, of how God was calling me to reflect on our relationship and, with His/Her help, to embrace and heal even the darkest hours. I had been working at Bethlehem Retreat Center seven days a week. For more than two years I had been under a great deal of pressure and stress, not only as Director, supervising its many programs, but also helping to run a fund-raising campaign to allow the purchase of the property. The Diocese needed to sell the Centre because of an unexpected financial crisis in the fall of 2000. This was a catastrophic blow to our community, as we had another eleven years to run on our lease.

After diligently looking and finding no suitable property from which to continue our successful ministry, we had to bite the bullet and purchase Bethlehem's entire property. The Diocese gave us only seven months to raise $1.3 million dollars. Many people from the Nanaimo community, as well as some who traveled from distant areas, counted on our counselling, educational, and spiritual programs. Educational and religious agencies also used the beautiful lakeside facility to help them serve their clients. Years of hard labour had gone into creating an inclusive and welcoming gathering place. Many of my skills, acquired over an adventurous and unusual lifetime, helped in providing this place of hospitality for groups and individuals. The future was now uncertain. A dilemma for sure!

If I said "yes" to a fund-raising, I would be doing something directly against my grain and I was already doing just too much of too much. Could we make bookings months in advance? I had to cancel a wedding scheduled nearly a year in advance because we might not still be at Bethlehem. My health was also an ever-present issue and I guess my age was too, for I was seventy-nine. I almost immediately knew two things. I had to pay attention to God's forceful nudge, and focus on sustaining my health and spiritual growth. This demanded that I travel the road to Duncan to work with Sister, for how long I did not know, but I needed help.

MY RANCH: A LEGACY

In late 1979 I was living in San Rafael, California with my husband, Hank. We had been in marriage counselling for several months. At the end of the session one day the priest asked me what I was going to do. I said, "Leave." He asked, "When?" I remember being exceptionally quiet and after a long silence finally was able to say, "Now, today." I got up and left. Alone! The next morning I walked out the door, leaving my home and marriage of over twenty-five years. I was leaving a whole way of life. Ultimately I became a Benedictine Sister and moved to British Columbia, which is now my home.

My entire life has been one of running from or toward something, with much circling and random movement. Always I have searched to understand who and why I was and where I was going. God called me to life and has continuously kept up this call, even though I was often deaf to its urging. My first feeling about God was one of fear, for God knew too much about me, and all of it was bad. My list of poor behaviours was long, and not to be forgotten nor forgiven, or at least that was how I understood the situation. No hope for me. As a child and throughout my life God has hounded me, and occasional church-going kept me asking questions that had no answers. I wanted to know more about this creator God who always seemed to be in the distance. My loneliness drove me to seek out God's unconditional love for me.

From about age seven I became aware that I was leading two lives at the same time, one Jill apparently going forward into life more or less appropriately to my age, but there was another Jill whose heart and mind were often in deep shadow, a shadow whose presence, while often hidden, still affected me deeply. My story is one of growing to make these two Jills congruent, blending into a single presence deeply loved by God. My childhood roots and years at home are of paramount importance in my search for a deepening of my relationship with God.

My birthplace was my introduction into a world of natural beauty. We lived in a ranch house near a lake, surrounded by enticing creeks, huge California live oaks, tall redwoods and many many other trees and shrubs. If I stood near our house and looked left, right, and up the hills to the mountain top, all I could see was forest, trees and a few meadows, a terrain so varied that there was a special drawing to see what was different just over the hill or down the creek bank or the deep forest beyond.

My paternal grandmother, Eliza Shepard, was Jack London's half-sister so I was part of a family with famous connections. In 1905 Jack London, who was a noted American author, started the purchase of the 1400 acre ranch in the area of the Sonoma Valley called The Valley of the Moon, about fifty miles north of San Francisco. London called his property "Beauty Ranch" and says of his lands: *I am rebuilding worn-out hillside lands that were worked out and destroyed by our wasteful California pioneer farmers. I am not using commercial fertilizer. I believe the soil is our one indestructible asset, and by green manures, nitrogen-gathering cover crops, animal manure, rotation of crops, proper tillage and draining, I am getting results which the Chinese have demonstrated for forty centuries.* He had learned about terracing or contouring hillsides while acting as a war correspondent in Korea in 1904.

My immediate family, first my Grandmother Shepard and then Dad, carried out the same principles of land management. If London returned to the ranch today, he would find that the land he used for crops is still productive and well managed. He could stand anywhere on the road, look up to the mountain, and see only those buildings present during his life, with the hundreds of acres on the wooded mountainside completely untouched. He would see the wilderness just as I remember it from my childhood. The trees, shrubs, meadows, and creeks that I roamed and enjoyed are still untouched and are now shared with thousands of people as they are a part of the Jack London State Park. Many of my unusual life experiences are a direct result of the privilege of calling this land home.

Jack London married Charmian Kittredge in 1905 and they made their home in Glen Ellen at Wake Robin Lodge, a house owned by Charmian's aunt. Among other books, London wrote *The Sea Wolf* while living there. The Londons traveled extensively, so they did not move to the cottage at the ranch until 1911. The cottage, one of the buildings on the Kohler and Frohling Ranch, was built in 1862 and was extensively renovated before Jack and Charmain moved in. They put in electricity and added a den for work space and to house Jack's 18,000 volume library. They fitted out one of the adjacent stone winery buildings for their dining room and kitchen, which made the old house quite comfortable. London had the carriage house renovated for guest rooms on one side and workers' quarters on the other. Many years later, my brother Jack and his family did further remodelling and lived in these same rooms. Farm equipment and wagons and carriages were stored in the center of the building.

As a child, I remember going into the den and seeing the old Dictaphone, thousands of books and a special cabinet to hold London's notes. This cabinet had many small drawers with labels on them so that Jack could easily find his notes on specific topics. I was so impressed by his special system that when I entered University I got a supply of 3 x 5 cards, and used them to write notes on the courses I took in Humanities; very useful when I had to write term papers.

London built the Wolf House, speaking of it as "a dream-house on my dream-ranch". It tragically burned down in August 1913, just days before they were to move in. Jack and Charmian continued to live in the cottage until his death there in 1916. Charmian stayed there until 1934 when she moved to the House of Happy Walls, which she built in 1919 using local field stones. It was designed as a museum, which it is today. Charmian traveled extensively after Jack London's death, leaving the running of the ranch to my Grandmother Shepard and later to Dad. Upon Charmian's death in 1955, Dad inherited the ranch and he has passed it on to the family.

Dad, Irving Shepard, and Mother, Mildred Ranker Shepard, both came to Glen Ellen, California as small children; Dad from Oakland and Mother from Greenville, both in California. They went to the tiny elementary school in Glen Ellen and then to Sonoma High School, some ten miles away. Dad went into the Navy during WWI while Mother spent some of those years helping at home.

My parents married in the fall of 1918 and went to live on the ranch in a home built by Grandmother Shepard. Mother and Dad spent all their married life in this house, enlarging it several times as our family grew. Mother continued to live there until her death. The ranch buildings are two miles up a private road from Glen Ellen, so we had no near neighbours. My grandparents lived in Glen Ellen and we had an extended family that made long visits to Charmian London or to my Grandmother Shepard. Charmian entertained many international visitors, Russian, Scandinavian, English, Australian, and Hawaiian as well as others from many distant parts of the world.

Mother's entire pregnancy with me was hard because Mother, who was only twenty-four, suffered severe pain from gall stones. She had surgery three weeks after my home birth on May 15, 1923. Given that this was over eighty years ago, it was major surgery requiring two weeks in the hospital, followed by an extended period of recovery. Consequently, Mother was not my primary caregiver during my first months.

I never knew I had a baby book until someone found it in Mother's drawer as we were going through her things after her death in 1981. Some of the information in the book verified old stories, but much of it was new to me. At a month I still weighed only four and a half pounds. I was a survivor from my earliest days; my zest and quest for a full life came extremely early.

June 2000. All my life I have remembered the story that I was so tiny they carried me around on a pillow. Well, I guess I needed gentle handling for I was underweight and no doubt a bit fragile, but the real problem caused by this low birth weight was that I did not bond to anyone. From my first moments I was alone, a bit different, and perhaps even a worry to my caregivers, especially Mother. The weather in California in May is usually warm so I did not need to be bundled up much. Mother nursed me at first but only when she put me on a bottle of cow's milk did I begin to thrive. No doubt, the struggle of these early months imprinted the message: "I made it, and I want all I can get out of life". For I surely have had boundless interests and energy all my life.

Mary Margaret was my given name and they called me Margaret. I am not sure when I picked up the name Jill, but it was early and I think it came from Aunt Charmian who thought it was cute to have Jack and Jill in the family. In school, I used the name Margaret but by high school was more and more often called Jill; I have continued to be Jill to this day. This was a split that was never fixed. On hearing of this split a friend told me that it is obvious that Jill is the inquisitive, playful child who wants to run free and that Mary Margaret was the child who had to behave. My first word was "Daddy" and it is revealing that Mother writes, "You wouldn't try to say Mama". Later Mother wrote, "I gave you an extra big hug and you ran to tell Daddy for you said, 'Mama'. So happy always smiling never crying, slept beautifully and very bright and lively." A protestant minister christened me at home on February 24, 1924.

In this book Mother goes on, "We love you so much dear little girl. You are a great joy to Daddy and Mother." Further on she writes, "Mother was very envious of Daddy because he was the favoured one which was only natural as he loved you and was able to care for you which Mother couldn't do on account of illness but Mother is well and I can do for you and get you to enjoy both Daddy and Mother now." This is an interesting insight into my relationship with Mother. It was almost a plea for the closeness that we never had. I cannot remember ever seeking out Mother for help, advice, or just closeness; we never developed that type of relationship. Some of the loneliness I have felt all my life no doubt came from lack of bonding. I have often

25

sought time alone, and have had no fear of being alone in large cities or even travelling to foreign countries by myself.

The entry in my baby book goes on, "No matter how long a time, you always remembered me and always were glad to see me. The cunningest thing you did was to always go to Daddy. Your little arms stretched to him calling 'Daddy, Daddy' and would refuse Mother. But after Daddy had taken you then you would lean over smiling and kiss Mother many times." Refuse Mother certainly stands out as I read this. It apparently hurt her deeply or Mother would not have written about it when I was still a toddler.

My earliest memory at about age three is of an event that took place at the house of my Grandma Ranker. We were upstairs and Dad started to gather me into his arms and carry me down. I said, "No, walk". I re-member just barely catching a hold of the rungs in the banister and going down the long staircase. I must have wanted Dad to know I was a big girl and probably wanted to show off. I was first voicing and no doubt developing my life-long sense of "I can do it".

This was the first of many examples of my taking command of a situation and doing it by myself. Even today I have the sense of exhilaration that comes from risk-taking, trying something new. Throughout my life, I have stepped out in faith when there is no visible way forward. It is one of my greatest strengths and speaks also of my courage. Being able to take risks, some fear-ful ones, has fostered my seeking out other cultures, other peoples, extensive traveling, and undertaking many different vocational directions.

My brother Jack, who was born in August 1921, was twenty-one months older. My baby book said that from my first steps I toddled after him. I overcame my slow start and grew rapidly into a strong child; it wasn't long before anything Jack could do, I could do too, or at least I would give it a good try. We had no neighbours, so Jack half-heartedly allowed me to be his play companion long before I was really able; many of the excursions we undertook were not checked out first with Mother.

Both of us followed our curiosity into all the vastness of nature around us. Certainly there were endless places to explore, to play games, and to collect treasures. Stones, worms, bugs and flowers or other great finds, including cookies, often filled my pockets. Jack seemed to know the answers to many of my questions. Sometimes he was very good about explaining the intricacies of some find but more often he was quick and short in his answers. Looking back I would say we probably got on better than most siblings because both of us had the same interests in nature and both just shucked off any hazards in our path. Jack was a good head taller and far stronger than I, so quite naturally he was the leader. He wanted a cooperative explorer and I wanted to be with him, though it took me years to be a real competitor. In the meantime I had to unconsciously learn to strike a balance between his need to be boss and my own desire for the same role.

I never liked dolls and can't even remember having any that mattered to me although I am sure I received many lovely ones as gifts. I do remember a tea-set of tin, painted in the Blue Willow pattern. I also remember and wish I still had a black stove with lids that lifted off and an oven that opened. Obviously Jack wouldn't want to play with girl's toys, so it was natural for me to start playing with his. My creativity showed up when I got into Jack's Lincoln Logs, those multiple cuts of brown wood that were grooved as real logs might have been. They could be fitted together to build houses, corrals and anything else my imagination could create. I was a good builder because I had an unusual amount of manual dexterity and, in fact, my fingers were as nimble as his. Jack's toys continued to be my main playthings as I could imagine and try to create many structures, especially when it came to erector sets.

When I was still less than three, someone drove me down to visit my Aunt Bunny, Mother's older sister in Los Angeles. Mother was very involved with the imminent birth of my brother Milo. I was a live wire and it was hard to contain me. I could easily avoid anyone in charge, run outside and away. They just couldn't catch me. Close to the house there was a garage, a woodshed and several large eucalyptus trees to hide behind. Perhaps the only sure way to care for me was to send me away. I have no recollection of the visit except for the drive home just at Christmas, a very scary adventure when the car got stuck in snow at the top of the Ridge Route.

When I was five I went to Aunt Bunny's at the time of my sister Joy's birth. I remember having to take dancing lessons and I hated it. I was shy and vividly recall being dressed in a one-piece pink leotard which was skin tight. I hated being there and fought against the lessons each and every time.

I wonder if my being away with others again kept me from bonding to Mother and perhaps even made me unsure about trusting those in charge. I know I was angry at being away from my ranch and playmate and when I returned, things were different. The two smallest children took up most of Mother's attention and my inevitable questions and need for time with her just didn't get recognized. No doubt Mother was under pressure, entertaining and trying to run a busy household. Jack and I were very hard to keep track of, skipping out to explore in the wild, regardless of the chance of being where we didn't belong. Gradually, we learned not to talk about our diverse activities so we could go further and further afield.

The conflict with Mother is a sore point even to this day. Mother first started to abuse me soon after I returned from my first stay with Aunt Bunny. No doubt she was finding it hard to care for a new baby and to have a grumpy, defiant three-year-old around. I never knew what would start Mother off, but the anger, the emotional tirades, and the physical abuse went on for years. I think I resented the switching the most because it took such a lot of time. We started to argue, Mother lost control and yelled at me. She sent me outside to pick a switch, and if it wasn't good enough, to get another. All the while she continued yelling. The switching was really painful; I jumped and danced about to avoid the lashes, which resulted in many red welts and stinging skin.

Today I realize that Mother's stress caused her to yell at me and of course I yelled back, stamped around, and probably struck out with my small fists. I am sure her spankings started out lightly, but gradually, with my rebellious ways and attitude, it came to a knock-down-drag-out fight. These fights became frequent and my behaviour deteriorated, as did hers, until it was just standard to expect a switching at any time.

Mother did not have a way of coping with my act-ing-out or at least not a way that ever worked. I needed her attention but wasn't getting anything positive so I withdrew, and just anticipated punishment and steeled myself for it. Our relationship was a disaster. The worst result of this abuse is that I did not have a mother who loved and protected me. I never had this at all, and it hurt. It made me feel unwanted and unloved through and through. As I got older I remember running out of the house and hiding, trying to get away from her cruelty. Mother's distress with me never was resolved and she remained highly critical of me even into my adult life.

March 2001. I was ashamed of my mother's los-ing it and very angry at her. I am beginning to un-derstand she parented my curious and independ-ent nature the wrong way. She wasn't able to keep her cool or manage to bring me into line without beating or yelling. The shame was so, so deep; I certainly didn't want anyone to know what she did to me. I heard over and over again I was the problem. Now I know differently.

The able me put on a steel jacket around the hurt me. My insides cringed, I was fearful, highly judgmental of myself, ashamed, and so just even being was difficult. The jacketed inner me was not growing at all but hurting, mixed up, and sometimes a mess. It did not get better as I got older because I did not have the tools necessary to penetrate the shell. Yes, I touched it at times, but was ashamed of the inner me and of the hate and fear directed to Mother that I didn't understand; stymied. So, jacketed, my pain more or less hidden, I went on with a measure of life. A heavy burden, but I need to acknowledge it and work it through now and let it go. I also realize I just tuned it out as much as possible, got away and as soon as I could, I went outside.

Dad bought a pony for Jack and me when I was about three. I was quite proud of my first ride alone and we stopped to show Mother how well I was doing. I had been on a lead rope, trying to adjust to the small saddle with my feet in stirrups instead of just sticking out as they did on the draft horses. The next thing I knew, the pony turned and ran for the barn. It was a long way off but he knew where it was and so, faster than you can imagine, he was running toward it as I screamed, "Daddy, Daddy!" The saddle slipped and there I was partly upside down hanging on for dear life. Yelling, crying, and scared to death. Dad had heard me, jumped in the car, and got to the barn where he quickly picked me off the pony and took me into his arms. It was so good to be there. The only real disaster was to my new shoes, scraped from dragging on the ground. I think this experience was more frightening than I let on. I continued to ride but only when necessary, like when a friend wanted to ride or we were going as a family to visit another ranch.

There was little Jack could do that I couldn't learn to do rather quickly. In those days I wore high-topped brown lace shoes around the ranch. I could get them on but not tie them securely. One day Jack was getting a lesson in tying shoelaces but Mother said I was too young to learn. She wouldn't let me stand beside him to follow along as she gave him directions. So I stood opposite him and closely watched what he was doing. To this day I tie my shoes backward or at least differently from most people.

"Wait for me!" was often my call to Jack. We both felt this huge ranch was ours and every free moment found us out exploring it and investigating anything new that came into our line of vision. Some of the paths that led us to where we wanted to go were often too difficult for me. I swallowed my fear or hid it deep inside, for surely it was there. I so much wanted to be with Jack; I always tried to keep up. "Fraidy cat" was a comment I didn't want to hear. A possibility of this taunt was enough to give steel to my body because not being his companion was not an option. Jack never tried to lose me when I was tiny, probably because he knew how much trouble he would get in when we got back.

When Jack went off to school I was just over four and, at least in my estimation, I was able to go any-where and felt safe by myself, so that's what I did. I have always had a good sense of direction and there were enough hills and trees to help direct me home.

I learned to read before I went off to school by watching Jack and listening carefully to him. I could read his easy books nearly as soon as he, and then began trying his more advanced ones. Mother liked to read to us but I hated being read to by her. I remember her reading a child's version of *The Prince and the Pauper* and I told her I had already read it. So she stopped and asked me to tell her the story, which proved I had read it. I didn't like her reading to us because she sat in the large Turkish chair with Jack on one side and me on the other; I was always in trouble for squirming and couldn't seem to sit still. More yelling! I just didn't want anyone to read to me, I wanted to do it myself.

2002. Freedom was and is an important theme in my life. As I look back, re-experience some of the feelings of early childhood, I know I always wanted to be on my own and do it myself, whether I could or not. I had an unquenchable thirst to know and experience anything going and was always expanding my horizons. I was intensely aware of everything about me; sensitive, I noted even the slightest changes as a season progressed. No doubt Mother felt that we were often in danger out in the wild, but neither Jack nor I anticipated problems of any sort, and couldn't care less about our clothes, or the time of our return. My curiosity made it obvious that I had to explore anything new on my own, touch it, and closely examine it from all sides perhaps even take it apart. Jack felt my need for such examinations either slowed him down to my pace, or he considered it a rejection of his ready answers. Both of us were impatient and self-directed and got in each other's way quite frequently. This being different started early so I was on my own much of the time. My strong will, insatiable inquisitiveness and later my bookishness held me in continuous conflict with, and often outside the bonds of family life. I soon felt like a misfit in my family. Freedom has its consequences.

Jack and I loved to walk the contours along many of the hillsides not far from our house. Jack London speaking of the property said: *I had noticed the way the soil was washed down the hillsides by the rains, and I determined to prevent that, which I did by grading the land, making it over into rolling contours and abrupt terraces...But the big thing about it is that by these new contours I keep the moisture in the soil.* When I was a child these terraces had lain fallow for years but we made a game of running up them, seeing how many steps we took before going up to the next level. Walking to the contours meant going down past the pink house where the workmen lived, along the path to the dump, then across the meadow and up along the crest. In early spring this was one of the best places for wild flowers like Mariposa lilies, Soap plant, Trillium, Wake Robins, Diogenes Lanterns (Chinese lanterns), Mission Bells, and endless others whose names I soon came to know.

From the time I was four or five, if I was upset at Mother, or if Jack was not home, I snuck off alone to the contours because I liked the quiet and vastness of the space. In northern California the hills and meadows are golden brown most of the year and the short grass has a soft, velvety touch. There were no houses or buildings visible on our ranch and I was all by myself, away from everyone and everything. From my vantage point I could look over across the valley, find the various vineyards and other landmarks, and just imagine what was going on in the houses there. It was such a peaceful place to be. I felt very comfortable warmed by the sun. After a battle with Mother I needed to be alone to put myself together and find peace; time to quietly reflect on the confusion there was in the family. I loved the space to roam and my wanderlust took me into the woods, searching for a spot to just sit and take in the signs brought on by the changing seasons, and observing how this affected the bushes and trees. I brought disquiet to paths in the fall when the maples and other trees had dropped their leaves and they crunched beneath my feet but otherwise the old leaves and needles made a soft and quiet path.

✠

September 2004. I had no introduction to God, or at least to a friendly God, for in my family we did not gather for prayer, or go to church together. Sunday school, which came later, did nothing to give me a sense of a loving God, or of God's involvement in creation. I sensed someone was in charge of things as seasonal changes and growth brought forth questions when I was very small. I had no one to answer my questions about why, how come, or what came next. Jack was too abrupt, others didn't seem to want to be bothered, or just didn't know how to answer such questions from a child.

It didn't take me long to begin to know that some questions just wouldn't get answered, so why ask? I now realize God communicated by giving me the ability to observe ever-changing natural sights before my eyes, the beauty in the silence and stillness when I was alone on the contours or in the depths of the forest. I have come to know that this sense of presence was how God called me and directed me in my early years. This powerful unspoken communication has been continuous throughout my life.

In a way, God was planting my feet in Mother Earth, a stable base from which to grow and experience life. The awe and wonder at the minutiae in nature ignited a spark in me which has continued to warm me throughout my whole life. There are always hidden wonders to search out. I think of the many pictures I took in Israel of flowers hidden among thorns, behind stones, peeking out of the dry sand, yet they caught my eye. Now I have the tools and my camera allows me to share the awesome beauty of the tiny flowers with others. My heart expands when I am in such close contact with my Creator, bringing peace deep within.

I have a long history with God, but not all of it is pleasant. It is easy for me, even today, to see myself snuggled down in bed, covers over my head, just pondering the words, "Forever and ever. Amen." They scared me to death. Somehow the forever gave me no hope at all because there was no end. I struggled with this concept night after night, tossing and turning, trying to understand. I was five or six years old when this idea became an operative part of my life's direction. My God was a punishing God who kept score. I was often a naughty child and Mother's words, "God doesn't like naughty girls", rang in my years whenever I was disobedient, which was most of the time. Constant repetition and many variations of the same message convinced me that God kept a list of everything bad that I did. I scared myself silly with those words. I knew that forever and ever meant that God's list would just get longer and longer. This list branded me, marked me forever.

September 20, 2002. This was no light understanding for me as a small child. God as a judge, erroneously reinforced in my child's mind so many times, allowed these simple words to really frighten me. Since God had a list of all my bad actions why would he want to give me something good? There was no hint about any sense of forgiveness or any erasures from the list. *Forever and ever* meant until the end of time, and there was no chance, no choice, I was already condemned. So, as far as possible, I just ignored discussion or thinking about God who was certainly no one with whom I wanted to develop a relationship. Even to this day I am jolted when I come to a prayer ending *forever and ever*. Not fully healed from that experience, I guess. No one ever had a hint of my fear of God. I just kept this secretly in my mind, never speaking of God at any time. I had questions galore, but no way to let them out. I have no idea when I realized that there is one Creator God. I put God the judge in an entirely different category from the Creator. They were not the same, in my young mind, and I am unaware of when I might have begun to put them together. My suspicion is that I was already an adult when this happened. This is an example, it seems to me, of the poverty one suffers from not knowing God early in life.

All children are full of questions but I also saw many wonders, and experienced some things that I could not put into question form. To be told "You will understand later on" was of no help. Later on I discovered books that were a wonderful help, and they remain so to this day. Somehow, one of the real lessons I learned at that time about how all creation came about and is interconnected, did not take God into account at all. How I wish it had. It would have enhanced my understanding of nature and given me additional reasons and responsibility to preserve all of God's natural gifts. One of the perks of living on a ranch was this chance to really relate to nature.

✠

Near the Pink House, just off the side of the road, was an old well not then in use, but filled by rain and drainage from the creek. We found two large snakes and many little ones in the well. I remember squatting

38

down, leaning over the rim of the rather large opening, reaching down to get the newborn snakes and taking them out and playing with them. There were about fifty tiny ones and two large snakes. I was never afraid of them, but when we got home one of us must have talked too much because the well was soon covered up. I can imagine that we could easily have fallen in. We were just too interested in the snakes to even dream of danger. Caution to the winds was our motto.

I constantly wanted to know more and more about the creepy crawlies, the snakes, anything that flew, always exploring and meticulously investigating all growing things. I remember moss with its tiny tendrils sticking up into the air; I could see when I blew on them that they were so fragile that my breath might be death to them. To me, death meant change; something changed and couldn't be the same again. So I learned that many things were fragile and required care when I inspected them. Picking up things and looking at their construction, I then took them apart piece by piece if I could. I remember picking a Mariposa lily and on taking it all apart, was aware that the parts were like those of other flowers; I wondered what made it a different colour. I was too young to understand, so I kept questions like that until years later. Once I took a good look at a newly sawn log and saw the skin and all the rings and wondered what they meant. The next time I came to a log, I was busy counting off the years.

September, 2003. If my knees allowed, I could walk to those exact spots today for fortunately they are still untouched by progress, though of

39

course the passage of years has made changes in them and in me too. God has given me many precious gifts, among them the years on the ranch. While the freedom of life on the ranch was formative and has been operative all my life, it was not until these last years of reflecting on my past that I was able to fully acknowledge the impact and richness of these experiences. I was much happier out in the woods than in the house. Nature, the adventure and the excitement of new finds, made me always want to escape from the house and see any changes around the ranch. Bad weather sometimes kept me indoors, but as soon as I could really read my other escape was into books and we had all kinds of books and magazines around.

One night Jack and I went to bed early, or so it seemed to Mother. We might have been just too quiet. Suddenly she threw back my blanket and found, much to her dismay, three baby mice along my waist; I was protecting and keeping them warm with my pyjama top. Jack had done the same. When Mother stopped screaming, we had to gather these small creatures up and take them back to the nearby field. We never did understand the fuss.

October 2002. The call to something more, to the challenge of doing new things or serving in new ways, has been answered because my feet are rooted in the stance of freedom I took so early. My deep sense of stability and the call, together, have allowed me over my lifetime to redirect my walk, the size of my step, and to take many risks.

I did not ask for this life but nonetheless it is here. It belongs to me and no one else. In the process of growing up I was touched, moulded, directed, and damaged in all sorts of ways and by many different people. Freedom to respond in new ways has been one of the greatest blessings God has given me. I would rarely give in just to conform, so there were and are many ups and downs in my life, very similar to the contours of my childhood landscape.

My first nurturer was Grandma Ranker. Among the happiest memories of my childhood were the times I spent with Grandma. She was a strong woman, a stern taskmistress who said things straight and true; she expected even small children to do the best they could. She had brought up five children, three of them girls, and had taught them good work habits. She was patient, and was delighted when I mastered a task quickly. Grandma was a steadying influence in my life. Mother often left me with Grandma for a few hours. Though not spoken of, this was a necessary and good balance to the abusive relationship with Mother, and gave Mother more time with the little ones.

Certainly having so much personal attention from Grandma helped me learn many of the usual household tasks. Being with her developed my sense of confidence and trust. One day, when I was less than six, I stood on a chair at the kitchen sink learning how to peel apples; Grandma didn't like to waste anything, and I had to learn to peel them thinly. I had a very sharp knife in my hand and rather quickly got the skill to peel well. I was delighted with myself. Mother came by to pick me up and I got yelled at for two things, standing on a chair, and using a sharp knife. Grandma got yelled at too, but she said that a sharp knife was less dangerous than trying to peel with a dull one, so I continued to show my new skill.

When I was about six, I begged and begged to kill a chicken; I had watched many times and just knew I could do it myself. There was a big oak chopping block, already a bit stained with blood with a notch to stretch the neck over. I placed the chicken's head more or less correctly on the block and gave it a good whack with the razor-sharp hatchet. Off went the head; I was lucky to get it with the first chop. The bloody hen ran away, stumbled, and flopped down the path because I was not strong enough to hold it. Grandma started to chase it, telling me that she didn't want it bruised, which was why I had to learn to hold on to it.

This is a prime example of Grandma's care about how one did a job. Grandma always gave second chances; a great help to a child who often wanted to do something before she had learned how. Grandma treated me like an adult, talking over which chicken to catch for the pot, and why, or which fruit was ripe enough for jam or which peas were fully mature. She taught me to use my common sense, and gave me plenty of chances to use my own head. Yet I remember when I was scared by a storm of thunder and lightning or by an earthquake, she let me crawl into her bed for safety.

When I was very tiny, Grandpa worked in his blacksmith shop in Glen Ellen. I liked to go in there, but sometimes I have to admit I was a bit scared as it was, at least to me, an enormous shop with all kinds of tools, a fire for forging iron, and very dim light. Sometimes Grandma sat in the car and I ran to the door to let Grandpa know it was time to go home. I would never have thought of going into such a place alone, but from the entryway I could see Grandpa, called out to him, and felt safe.

One day it was evident from the smell in the kitchen that a skunk had died far back in the cellar at the lowest point of the house. Grandma tried to get it out with the rake; she couldn't. She needed my help and used her flashlight to light my way. Her confident urging, "You can get it Margaret, just turn your rake a bit", and her positive tone helped. Grandma took over as soon as possible and buried it. She used her strong washing soap to wash me from head to toe but I smelled of skunk for quite awhile.

My grandparents had about five acres, a large fenced orchard and garden, as well as two chicken houses up on the hill. The vegetable garden had oodles of variety so everything we ate was home grown. There was always weeding needed and my little hands got good and grubby but I felt successful as I cleared a patch. Grandma grew many kinds of fruit so I learned to evaluate the correct ripeness of the fruit and how to handle it carefully as I put it into jars.

Chickens were the main source of meat for Grandma and Grandpa. After the visit to the chopping block Grandma doused the chicken, neck first, into the water, then put it on a stack of newspapers and picked off the feathers. I had my nose right down there as she removed the innards. It wasn't long before I wanted to try this on my own, but I had to wait some years before I could to do the job by myself. By then I had learned how to remove the gallbladder and the lungs. I knew chicken anatomy. Best of all was when we killed an old hen and found eggs in various stages of development. Some yolks seemed quite large before the white showed up. Those with the soft shell, nearly ready for laying, were also of great interest to me. Grandma did not allow any shenanigans when one was working; she demanded a careful job each and every time. I can still cut up a whole chicken quickly. She taught me to work efficiently.

Delicious mincemeat from an English family recipe was made in late fall. When it came time for the hard liquor, we went to the bar in Sonoma. Grandma took me inside; it was fairly early in the morning and I don't remember any patrons. It was just a small space beside the movie theatre. She sat up on the bar stool, as did I. I can imagine the bartender was surprised to see this little old lady (probably in her 60's) with her hat squarely on her head, asking to have a taste of his best brandy. She said she wanted a bottle for her mincemeat. He graciously gave her a taste and she thought it good and bought a quart. Mother found out about my being in the bar and you can imagine her reaction.

I realize that, while I lived with my family on the ranch, my real direction about how to live life came from my Grandma Ranker. She was the one who provided a safe haven no matter the storms all about.

44

I knew I could walk into her house and feel secure, loved, and cared for; I was always warmly welcomed. I will be eternally grateful for the deep relationship I had with Grandma and I was, in some sense, her special charge. Obviously, I gobbled it up when I was so young. Grandma had to have known or sensed the abusive relationship with my mother but she never spoke of it directly to me at any time and I cannot recall ever bringing up the subject.

I strongly believe that Mother's difficulty with control developed only after she married and had children. Mother just wasn't able to cope with her strong mother-in-law and Charmian, who were so closely involved in our lives. Grandmother Shepard had only the one son and Charmian never had children. Of the two women who dominated Mother's life, I preferred being with Grandmother Shepard as I got older and went places with her. I do not remember being involved with Charmian off the ranch property.

April 28, 2002. My life has always been one of searching, a continual search but I could not always ask the right questions. I often searched for what I didn't have, as I sensed my lack of peace and safety. If I had to picture myself I would draw me far away from others in the immediate family and all those who lived with us. Some family friends said that I was always different, even asking me as a small child, "Why are you so unlike your brothers and sister?" The family expectations of decorum and dress were in the forefront of my mind; be prompt, clean and properly dressed.

My searching has not been negative but positive. I have made many wrong moves in trying to find myself, but the wavy up and down shows that the long pattern has had a positive upsurge. I am afraid to write this, but I must; today I got in touch with my fear that I could not do all I need to do to find my place before I die.

Growing Hurts

Our house had three bedrooms, a bath and a half, a large kitchen, and very large living and dining rooms with a fireplace in each. We mostly burned eucalyptus as we had groves of it and it made a good hot fire. When I was old enough to leave my cradle Jack and I shared a room with twin beds. When our brother Milo came along, remodelling enlarged the bedroom and the boys had bunk beds and I a single one.

Dinner was often a time of upset in our family. If we had guests, the expectations for behaviour were high. But at family meals Jack and I both did a lot of things that brought some angry words from our parents. We had active feet and liked to get each other's attention by kicking; we might also try to eat the best from someone else's plate or actually give them a bit more of something we didn't want to eat. Sometimes we got away with it; other times we were sent off to our room. I didn't know when to give up or stop arguing, and would carry it on too long and off I would go.

Off and on Dad and Grandpa Ranker, if called upon, worked in the ranch shop, which was in a big stone winery building used for repairing and storing some of the farm machines. Grandpa let me watch, and sometimes I could pick up the bellows and use it to stir up the fire to the right heat. It was fascinating to watch an iron horseshoe be placed in the fire, gradually glow red, then be picked out with tongs, laid on the anvil, and hammered into shape. Grandpa dipped it into a bucket of water; a mighty gust of steam went up high, and made a hissing noise. If the fit wasn't just right, back into the fire it went and he further adjusted the shape. Grandpa made us a teeter-totter, merry-go-round and slide as well as fine lamp frames and candle holders out of wrought iron.

Shortly after Joy was born, Dad enlarged the office off the front porch and remodeled it into a bedroom for Joy and me. It was a real downer for me to have to move out of Jack's room when I was seven. The end of an era, for it was harder for Jack and me to get up at the same time and meet outside or even to plan our days.

Joy and I continued to be stuck with each other until I was about thirteen and we no longer had a maid. The Guest Ranch opened, and this brought a different balance to our lives. I took over the maid's room; Joy kept the larger room. At last I had my much-needed privacy. My new room was small, with a tiny closet; just space enough for a single bed up against the window and a desk and chair. But it was mine and I could lock the door, though only with a skeleton key. I wove a blue

·and white cotton rug for the floor beside my bed and also made a large block print design on white muslin curtains for my one window. The design was of a deer drinking from a stream with trees in the background. It was about 8 x 10 inches, hard to ink and block so that it looked even. I was glad when I finished and quite proud of it as it took far more patience than I usually had!

November 2004. Thankfully I finally had my own space. I realize that from earliest days I needed time and place to be alone. This need to have my own space or to be alone in the outdoors is still with me and terribly important to my being able to live a more balanced life.

ALONE

True aloneness
no sound heard

Loved   searched out
just for myself

Invited to come
called
be with

Place my steps
in those
of Jesus

I have no memory of the precipitating event but some-where between ages six and seven I ran away to Grand-ma Ranker's house. It was a long two miles through trees, across meadows and gradually to the backyards of houses near hers. There was no path and I didn't want to walk on the road, as someone might see me. I re-member climbing a fence or two and ultimately ending up in Grandma's back yard, much to her amazement. She asked me to show her how I got there and we went up to the chicken yard and I pointed out the fence I had climbed. I was crying or at least sniffling, with torn clothing and scratches over every exposed part of my body. I must have had a good sense of direction because as I look today from the meadow through the hill and over to her house it was a frightening feat for such a small child. Grandma didn't have a phone so she got the car and took me back home, where more trouble awaited me.

My reflection of this event, still strong in my mind, says I had on a dress and my low shoes and so got many burrs in my socks. When I reached Grandma after the horrendous struggle of getting there, I was very tired and scared. She comforted me, clutching me to her with her apron forming a good hankie for my tears and runny nose. Welcomed, safe, but it did not change the need for an immediate car trip home. I have no idea whether or not anyone missed me but probably not, as no one was out looking for me.

As I said before, Grandma didn't take sides. If I did something that was wrong at her house she would let me know it in her own way and didn't report it back to Mother. There was a real sharing with her from the time I was tiny. She encouraged my endless questions and somehow put up with my squirming, quick, inquisitive bent. I knew I belonged with her and always felt safe. The loneliness disappeared when I was with her.

I know Mother judged me as a rebel and quite a mouthy one. She found something wrong every time I went into the house. It might be dirty shoes or clothes, or running when I should have walked, or just being late, or having messed up in some way. Mother's message was, if you could do it the wrong way you would. The haranguing was continual and I grew to expect it. My lying started someplace along the line by saying, "Yes, I did", when I really didn't, just so Mother would stop. Actually, as I look back now, Mother had some false standards for children living on a huge ranch. Even if I give her the benefit of the doubt and acknowledge that I did some dangerous things, she still got out of control.

From the time I was still under four, on until I left for college, there was heavy physical and emotional abuse. In fact, throughout Mother's life I was always out of step with what I should be doing. All her life Mother criticized me, always wanted to know my business, or pointed out my shortfalls regarding how I decorated my home, took care of the children and on and on; hard to take. The abuse made me a split person, a stranger in my own skin. My private self carried deep shame but in front of guests and even some family my mask showed everything was okay. In some ways I thought people could see deeper than is possible.

Sometimes our interaction was just awful but it seemed that if I did not cry Mother stopped more easily. I learned to suppress my real feelings, as I was afraid they would come across too strongly. Even when I wanted to cry I could not because I used, "You can't hurt me" as a way of controlling Mother. I clearly know that there was no one to talk with about any of these events; I just stuffed it down for many years. The scars from these childhood punishments were deep and I can thank God they are now healing, but as I write honestly and truthfully I need to say that their impact on me and my life was huge.

February 2001. I had bad thoughts, ugly ones and was ashamed of them too. I wanted Mother gone, hurt, dead, or at least someway out of my life. Like many children I expressed my hatred and fear of her by acting out and I became a rebel. Always put down. I wished I could act better. I also remembered how hard it was for me to take some things in, and I often let a mask come up and then I could carry on as if I was not hurt. It's time to start giving up the pattern of shame. It has been so long; really all my life, but I no longer need to be ashamed, as I have led a rather good life, and have helped and supported others in a wide variety of ways.

Dad wasn't able to help in my relationship with Mother. He seemingly could not stop her from the emotional abuse and often was not present when

I was beaten. Dad was caught in a trap and somehow, even when small, I sensed that he could not help in certain ups and downs presented to little Jill. Weak and capable at the same time, something found in all of us. I felt Dad's absence in the punishment side of my upbringing; his involvement might have helped. Many other aspects of his personality and abilities as a dad seemed to overcome this weakness, at least in my eyes and I always related to him well.

Now I know that Mother just wasn't able to handle small children, a busy household with a maid, and all the outside criticism she got. Mother lived under a great deal of tension and apparently she just didn't know where to get help. Even if I might, in the slightest way have been the cause, the punishment was just harder than I could bear. So I am beginning to know where my feisty and strong nature came from and why it was my saviour.

I was a survivor from my earliest days on earth. Eventually I did not have to struggle for survival because the patterns just became a deep part of me and I was quick, sure, mouthy and apparently untouched. I took the guff even though inside I might be shattered and coming apart at the seams. My quickness of mind, and ability to get lost about the ranch allowed me to avoid a lot of pain. My feelings were jammed down and covered over so deeply that now I ask the question, "Where was the real Jill?" Not only did others not know me, but I now realize I didn't know myself either, though I did have the ability to get through life. A hell of a way to live.

Caught up in survival, my mind, body, even my spirit were free to roam on the outside, but were locked up on the inside. It was a good thing I had so much energy and spunk. Having to keep myself locked up was terribly draining and took a toll on my health. Because of the abuse I persisted in finding freedom wherever I could. How was it then that I ended up in a convent and taking a vow of obedience? What strange work would God do in me to bring me to that place?

When I hear people say I am a very generous and giving person I often don't hear the words or accept them. Of course, I don't hear good things about myself easily. This is still a growing edge for me. I think it may be nearly automatic for me to resonate with people with troubles. For many, I am a safe place to unload so I try to listen and be available. I realize how many hurting people there are out there and I want to do all I can to make their life a bit better than my own has been.

January 6, 2004. My intensity seems to be diminishing; I seem to have slowed down a lot. I spend much more time by myself during the day and into the evening. I not only want this aloneness but I seek it out. Aloneness is absolutely necessary so I can hear and feel. Lonely still relates to God, a lack of awareness. Loving and allowing myself to be loved is a problem. It's like I don't pick up enough of the blessings all around me. What does it mean to let others love me? I'm not sure, yet change is coming here. The quietness within is

54

much more consistent and persistent. I know I can reach out to others and I do sometimes.

I think this is a physical change in intensity brought about by an understanding of how I am changing. I used to live full tilt so nothing would be lost or missed, and I always felt vulnerable. Now I am quiet to hear, to evaluate, and have time to reflectively respond. Listening for a call or a direction seems more important to me now, and I listen so as to be able to respond to nuances of call.

I was in Duncan and my Director suggested I sit before the crib. I was just present there alone in the chapel, and for a long time, getting deeply quiet. The Blessed Mother picked up baby Jill and held her...speechless, deep. Powerful. Awesome. Presence. For a long time I was just there. Even as I went back to my room the powerful peace of the moment caught me, a Mother's love, healing me.

I was not more than five when Dad and I had gone in the truck to Sonoma where we went into the huge corner hardware store, which was loaded with all kinds of tools and other things farmers or their wives needed. The store was rather dark, with only string lights dropping down from the ceiling. It also had an added attraction, a gum dispenser sitting on the cash counter. That got me. When we went out to get in the truck, I had a hard time climbing into my seat, my legs were short, and Dad gave me a hand up. You can imagine my shock and shame when a package of gum rolled out of my sweater onto the floor. Dad saw it immediately and asked me where I got it. He knew I didn't have money for a purchase and hadn't asked him for any. I 'fessed up rather quickly. Dad took my hand and we went back to see the store owner. I returned the gum, telling him I had taken it without paying for it. That shame was acute and long lasting. There was no other hardware store in town so if I needed to make a purchase there I got someone else to go in for me. I think it was over thirty years before I had enough guts to go back to that store. It cured my light fingers.

One day Grandmother Shepard gave me a penny as we stopped at Poppy's grocery. You could buy a lot of candy for a penny but that day I put my penny in the slot machine. I was lucky and hit the Jackpot with pennies all over the floor, such luck. Mother waited while I picked them up and added them to the scooped-out ones from the tray. In all, I had well over a dollar, a huge amount. My joy was quickly shattered as Mother made me turn all the pennies over to the grocer. I knew this wasn't right as they didn't belong to him, but Mother said that was what had to happen so my luck turned into shame. This was one of those frequent times when I couldn't understand the reason for the decision Mother made. Since there was no discussion about it, just the order to do it, that only added to my confusion.

March 1, 2001. It took years before I could begin to let others really know me. I was unsure, did not trust others with my past escapades. I felt that if they knew me they might be disgusted, especially if they had a clue about what shameful thoughts and other things I kept inside. I felt that they wouldn't like me or talk to me and the last state would be worse than the first.

Today I know it was false guilt and shame. I feel safer than ever before and can begin in a real and healthy way to just let it go. Proof is all around me that I have no need to be ashamed at this time, so I can choose not to let the horror of past events be such a large factor in my daily life. It's like I need to carry lighter burdens because there is still so much I can do if I am free inside. If I get the false shame off my back I will be able to do those things asked of me. Lord, may this be... and with your help it can come about.

✠

Christmas was a special time at our house and some Christmases were definite standouts. When I was about three-and-a-half and Jack was two years older, each of us got cycles. Mine was a big three-wheel bright red tricycle and Jack's was a small bike. We always opened presents on Christmas Eve so just about dawn on Christmas Day we got up and started out. We had only one thing in mind, to ride away to a real adventure. We went down the hill and to the bottom of the road where it turned toward Charmian's house. It was a terribly long trip, about a quarter-mile, so for both of us it was a workout. Of course, Jack was stronger but as we turned to go home, probably because of hunger, he found the going up the hill as hard as I did. We got off the cycles and started trudging home. Someone noticed we were missing so Dad came to our rescue and our tired legs got a ride home.

Other Christmases, from about the age of seven Jack and I had to sing a few carols, or recite some special piece, or play the piano before we could open our presents. I know we speeded up our little fingers and tried to finish quickly so we could get to the presents. Christmas always meant a large crowd of guests, usually Grandmother Shepard's or Charmian's.

Many wonderful and interesting folk were part of my early life on the ranch. There was a large extended family and we called most of them Uncle or Aunt when we were children, though they were really not relations at all. Uncle Ham was a special friend of mine who was quite old, older than my grandmother. He liked my company and on many occasions I remember us sitting on either the steps to the front porch or the back porch. Uncle Ham would take out a steel pocket or kitchen knife, cut an apple in half, and scrape it. The use of a steel knife and the acid in the apple gave the apple an unusual taste that I liked. If I was good and not too wiggly I could eat the scrapings off the blade of the knife. Never got cut! He must have died when I was about five.

My Grandmother Shepard was someone to grapple with. She was a very strong, able woman and though slight in stature, in some ways was threatening to small children. She was born in the late 1860's, married very young to a man more than thirty years older than she. He had been a captain in the Civil War. He was a lawyer and influenced my grandmother to read law. She had one son, my father.

Whenever we went to visit Grandmother Shepard she seemed to have several guests, so this meant we had little time alone with her. Her stairs were a delight to small children as they curved and had a wide banister, and on occasion we used to slide down it. A no-no. Tommy Burns, her niece, took over watching us, and was an especially fine cookie cook. There was a great place to play in the creek and in wooded areas nearby.

Political and local affairs were always of interest to Grandmother. She was a very active and talented woman and was appointed by the Governor of California to organize the efforts of relief organizations after the 1906 earthquake in San Francisco. This involved her coordinating the work of the US Army, Red Cross and Salvation Army in the area. She was active in the American Legion Auxiliary founded after WWI, eventually becoming national president of that organization in the 1920's. There is a picture in a family album showing Grandmother at her desk in her office in Washington, D.C. On the desk is a picture of Jack and me when we were about five and three. She was also involved in the organization for wives of Civil War veterans. She was a spokesperson for wounded or ill ex-soldiers who needed support to get their just due from the Department of Veterans Affairs both in California and nationwide. She was also a spokesperson for farmers from the Petaluma region and one day I went with her to visit Governor Friend Richardson in Sacramento. I was about six and really upset, as he wanted me to sit on his knee. I am sure he could tell I was disgruntled and I got down quickly.

I knew her as a person who was home one day and the next day was perhaps in Florida, Europe, or anyplace else some special interest or need took her. She was always working for justice. With Grandmother Shepard I just followed along and often I was the only child with her. Grandmother always had someone drive her so when riding along I had her full attention and got good explanations to my questions. She expected me to sit quietly and listen when she stopped to see someone or had other business. I realize that her whole life was one of business and busyness. She was an independent woman and could talk with nearly anyone on their level. Since she had no family responsibilities she was readily available to work with others and their problems. It was also apparent to me that she was a generous, strong woman and talked with men as an equal, something that was not possible for Mother or Grandma Ranker as they were more homebodies.

Sonoma was a quiet town; only a few thousand people lived there and we knew nearly everyone, certainly all those who ran the stores. When I was about ten I heard that Mr. Henry Lordeaux, an electrician, shot and killed another merchant, something to do with adultery, whatever that was. I happened to be with Grandmother when someone took her to Santa Rosa to visit the jail where they held Mr. Lordeaux. I went right along with her and, accompanied by a sheriff, we walked down the stairs and into a long hall with cells on both sides. I remember being scared a bit as I had never seen a cell block even in a movie and didn't know what to expect. Grandmother visited with Mr. Lordeaux at his cell door, talking to him through the bars.

She wanted to see him because he had been doing some work for her and though it was too early to bill her, she felt he might need money; she wrote him a check. She often seemed to go the extra mile and I have always remembered her generosity in these kinds of situations. Later on, because of the circumstances of the crime they dismissed the charges against Mr. Lordeaux.

The other part of the story was that Mother was very upset because I had gone down to the jail cell; she was angry with Grandmother and of course with me. Mother was helpless to prevent these excursions; if I was with Grandmother Shepard I just went where she did. I think I picked up this going the extra mile from Grandmother's example and I have often helped people caught in jams. Because of Grandmother Shepard's many contacts our life was certainly fuller than that of most children.

Over the years some family members have remarked that I have a lot of Eliza in me and I think this is true. I too have always had an interest in business, a good understanding of money, am a justice bug, and a rather strong minded person. No doubt my taking off from teaching and going out to work for the Lord as a volunteer was akin to the things Grandmother did. She was a warm person, with a smile and quick interest in everything that was going on. However I do not remember her ever giving me a hug, or showing other signs of affection, nor do I remember that she did so with other family members. Her warmth and interest just came across in other ways and made her approachable by nearly anyone. She had a sharp eye for detail and an ability to get to the point quickly. She was an excellent card player and especially loved bridge. At Grandmother's I was often a fourth at whist and when auction bridge came in I immediately played that as well. If as a partner you made a major blunder you would hear about it, but she was quick to forget and get on with the play. I am still a bridge hound but now I play it on the computer.

One night, in the fall of 1939, Grandmother came to the door of the porch where we were playing cards and I remember her saying, "Good-bye" instead of "Good-night". She just stood at the door, not coming out as if this was no special occasion at all. The next morning the phone rang and it was Jan Narvaez who asked me to get Dad. I asked her if Grandmother had died, though I did not know she was that ill. Grandmother not only had heart trouble but also was a diabetic who often forgot to take her insulin. As we left her funeral there were by far more people outside the chapel than inside, with flowers covering the whole lawn of the funeral home. She certainly was well known and missed. Her ashes now are under the same rock as Jack London's, although with no marker.

I remember Aunt Charmian from my earliest days. Around the ranch she often wore riding pants and boots and usually a saucy hat and some bright scarf about her neck, summer or winter. She was petite, had beautiful white teeth, and was always using her hands for emphasis when she talked. She was flamboyant, different from the other adults I knew. I felt uncomfortable around her as I sensed she felt children had their place and it seemed as though I might often be out of mine. She was a conflicting influence in my family life. There was unpleasant tension in the family when she was around, as she expected Mother to run a well managed household and Jack and I did not always behave appropriately; there were so many ways we could get out of control on the ranch. And we did. We have some moving pictures of Charmian out in her garden and also riding on a horse, as well as many snapshots. Charmian was the author of several books; one, *The Log of the Snark*, detailed the trip the Londons took in 1907 to the South Seas. In my early childhood Charmian entertained quite frequently, especially in summer. She travelled extensively so was often away visiting friends.

In my late teens Charmian moved over to the House of Happy Walls, which she built so it could be a museum at the end of her life. On a clear day, we could hear her playing her grand piano for the sound carried a long way; it was often Chopin. Her staircase walls were unique, covered in Tapa cloths against which were displayed long sharp spears from Samoa. Other large white Tapa cloths were made into drapes for some of the windows. Halfway up the stairs there was a look out that one could access by pulling a small panel that seemed to be part of the wall. One could stop and sneak a look down to the living room from there, without others knowing about it. Charmian also had a secret staircase from the library up to a closet in her bedroom. Jack and I knew it existed and one day, while over there with Dad, we searched and searched for it. Finally, we noticed a discrepancy in the way the bookcases lined the wall, and discovered that one of the bookcases swung out and was a door. We opened it, then scrambled up the spiral stairs and arrived in the closet in Charmian's bedroom. Charmian wasn't yet living there and I have no memory of trying this stunt when she did reside there. However, it was a great treat to have such a special place that we could visit.

The effect of these two strong women, Charmian and my Grandmother Shepard, on me was a real mixture of contradictions. It was difficult living with their expectations yet the strength evidenced by their individual accomplishments was a positive inspiration to me. Charmian was her own person, unique, sometimes quite a loner and at other times a wonderfully happy person with a gift of hospitality. She gave me many opportunities to meet and talk with people from many walks of life, particularly foreigners, which no doubt early on broadened my own horizons. I particularly remember some of her Scandinavian friends and many years later relished a few days in Copenhagen when my plane schedule allowed a three-day stopover. Charmian also influenced me through her experiences of world wide travel and adventure, both with Jack London, as they cruised on their boat the Snark, and her stories of many other travels. It is interesting that Grandmother Shepard influenced me by her service to others, her excellent mind, and strong will, while Grandma Ranker fed me from her gentle and deep example of good mothering and I found safety with her.

Charmian owned the ranch and first Grandmother Shepard and then Dad managed the day-to-day running of the ranch. They also took care of all the London book contracts and any other business. I have said that Jack and I both thought the ranch was ours and indeed as children we did not even know of the actual ownership or other business arrangements. The ranch was where Dad worked and we lived and that was that.

When Charmian died Dad inherited the ranch. Mother and Dad generously gave the State of California thirty-nine acres including the cottage where Jack and Charmian lived, the Wolf House, the House of Happy Walls, and all the other ranch buildings except our house. With other portions of the ranch purchased by the State, today the Jack London Park has over eight hundred acres and has thousands of visitors each year. Dad held on to about two hundred acres for family use. The vineyard planted on our Shepard family portion is very productive; the soil and location are especially good for red grapes such as Cabernet, Merlot and Zinfandel.

CREATORS

Together we create
God and me
awesome task

Allow myself to be with
be co-creator

Just standing there...
being...
waiting until called to move
Chaos is mostly mine
life's reality

I am whole
With God's presence

BECOMING ME

Life on the ranch allowed me heaps of freedom, some given or approved by my parents, but most just taken. For example, Mother often picked us up at the bus stop but if she was late we would try to hide from her and walk home. If Mother called to us we didn't answer. Jack and I would be lying face down in one of the meadows or hiding out in some of the woods. Then like two scamps we resumed our way home, taking a good long time to walk the two miles. We told tall tales about why we had not heard Mother calling. Those were special times seeing animals on the way, exploring in the woods, pretending, even scaring each other. They were times of freedom, times of developing our independence and both Jack and I grew up as very strong, independent adults.

Just up the first hill after entering the ranch, piles of rocks stretched for several hundred feet along the south side of the road that crossed a large meadow. The stones thrown out of the roadbed by those driving cars, or earlier, horses, made an interesting spot for exploration. We knew there were lots of creepy crawlies in among the stones and we climbed up the pile to scare them out of their hiding places. Investigating the stones stuck in my memory and fifty years later I wrote a story related to those stones and the magic they contained. I wasn't afraid of animals, snakes included, but was always startled if I came on them unexpectedly especially if they shot out of the stone piles.

On our ranch there are two large silos that have special memories for me. We climbed clear to the top rather easily but it was the depth of the silo that got me. We jumped down in to look around, but things didn't turn out quite as I expected. Either Jack abandoned me deliberately, or he was just trying to run ahead to scare me, but I wasn't tall enough to grasp the bar that would let me climb out, not even with a running jump. Cry and shout I did. Jack was nearby and eventually he jumped down and I climbed up on his shoulders, grabbed the bar and got out. This upset was the beginning of trouble between me and Jack. He had a need to keep the upper hand in our relationship; I was always testing it.

We frequently went to the lake that was only a quarter of a mile up a rough dirt road from the house. There were wonderful oak trees along one bank, and a boathouse with a canoe, a rowboat and an Alaskan kayak. We jumped into the water from the pier jutting out into the lake to avoid the muddy bottom. A grove of redwoods surrounded a large picnic table with a barbeque in case chicken or hamburgers were on the menu. Foreign visitors often brought spicy fish and cheeses. If Charmian was entertaining she brought her beans, wonderful kidney beans with special sauce. Sourdough French bread from the local bakery was nearly always included. Children had a nearby table that suited us just fine.

Jack and I often went to the lake alone. The dam at one edge was about thirty feet high, not too wide, and the top surface had worn over the years so it was covered with gravel bits and debris which made walking across it difficult. Of course we weren't supposed to walk it but we did. One time Jack gave me a push and over the edge I went. Thankfully the dam was of rough concrete so I found foot- and hand-holds and got out. I just let my clothes dry on me. Jack and I were often competing; he always had the upper hand and began to take advantage of it. Sometimes I didn't know what I was getting into but I needed to be with Jack, so I just took a risk that all would work out.

Jack and I often took a jar of lemonade, a sandwich, and fruit and off we would go to the creek. We went to one special place, put the jar in the water to keep cool, and proceeded with our work. Usually it was to build a dam and watch the water rise. My adeptness in envisioning a dam and in placing the stones helped create a sturdy dam. Then slowly we would take it apart, stone by stone until suddenly the weight and rush of the water would destroy the dam in one fell swoop. This was a moment of Wow, I could control a bit of nature. One day I was not careful and looked down to find the water clear over the tops of my high-topped leather-laced shoes. I changed quickly into others when I got home. Fascinated by running water then and still, I have enjoyed taking pictures of many streams and waterfalls on my journeys.

Summer vacations were often special in our family. I remember several visits to Capitola, a small town on the coast about sixty miles south of San Francisco. Jack and I liked to go down to the pier and fish before breakfast. I was always good at catching them, so fish was often available for breakfast. From there we went to Yosemite, and camped. "Margaret, watch out!" was Dad's loud call as I fed chocolate to a bear in Yosemite park. We had stopped to look at the mother and cubs and offered them Hershey bars. The mother wanted more and reached out with her paw for the piece still in my hand. Her paw scratched my face and Dad grabbed me, pulled me back to safety, and into the car; we watched the bears from there. No signs told us not to feed the animals.

Sometimes we would go up the Redwood Highway and often ate crabs and seafood as we went up the coast. I remember getting sick and now realize I have an allergy to seafood. On these camping trips I used to sleep on one of the car seats with a blanket as did Jack. Dad might gather some boughs and put them under his and Mother's sleeping bags. Both my grandmothers came on one trip. They had blankets just tossed on the ground. I remember laughing in the morning when Jack and I rose early and saw them in bed, both with their hats on! I don't know what they were trying to keep out of their hair. Both grandmothers had long hair which they put into single braids for the night.

70

These vacations were all during the Depression era, before I was twelve, as after that Dad was involved in the Guest Ranch. Since the grandmothers were sometimes with us and Dad was always present, Mother was a bit easier on me.

✠

San Francisco was "the City" that drew us not only because of its diverse cultural offerings, but also because we did such exciting things as take cable car rides and travel both ways by ferry in all kinds of weather. When I was tall enough to reach up and grab the pole I could hang on to the outside of the cable car, and sometimes was even allowed to ring the bell. The city was two to three hours away, depending on whether or not we made the ferry at Sausalito. Going to San Francisco meant I had to wear properly shined or patent leather shoes, socks well pulled up, a hat, and white gloves, with a replacement pair if they got dirty. Of course, walking in the stores without handling anything at all was a mark of proper decorum, sometimes hard for me with my curiosity. In those days if you shopped for clothes, even for a seven to ten year old girl, you and your mother sat down and a lady asked how she might help. She went inside to the racks, and brought out a selection of four or five items. Then, if those were not suitable, brought others. This was the way we shopped until after WWII. I guess there were other stores with not quite so much help, but I didn't know them. There were also catalogues, but they were for the men's work clothes or our rubber boots.

As we got older we went to San Francisco to visit museums, Chinatown, and also to go to plays or musical events. Often we had lunch at an ethnic restaurant and I especially liked going to Chinatown. My first musical event was a concert in the Geary Theater by Yehudi Menuhin when he was about twelve, and I was about six. His encore was "Flight of the Bumblebee". What a delight to all the audience. Apparently it made a lasting impression on me as I asked to take violin lessons, which I started in sixth grade and continued until my third year in high school. When Jack and I were quite young we loved to go to the De Young Museum as well as to the Japanese Tea Garden in Golden Gate Park. The De Young Museum was quite large and in addition to its permanent displays of art and other exhibits, it offered many special events. I remember visiting a show of Van Gogh paintings brought from Holland, and also a fabulous Egyptian collection that was on tour world wide. The Palace of Legion of Honor right out on the bluff overlooking the Golden Gate was particularly interesting to children because of its many sculptures by Rodin. His famous sculpture, The Thinker, is only one of many purchased for the museum which honours the California men killed in World War I. From this area you can look back at the whole Bay and see the bridges, Alcatraz, and Mt. Tamalpais though sometimes you only see the famous San Francisco fog which rolls in silently, particularly in summer.

When I was in high school we went to San Francisco for stage plays and it was my privilege to see all the major plays between 1936 and the first years of WWII. Helen Hays, Gertrude Lawrence, and many others came to "the City"; I actually saw Hays in Victoria Regina three times. The San Francisco Symphony was another event we often attended as we had friends who were supporting these musical concerts even during the Depression. Music filled our lives and I got to know quite a repertoire of music as I also listened to the radio and later to phonograph records. My hearing loss in these last years has greatly interfered with my enjoyment of musical events, even records, tapes or CDs, as there is always something in the way.

I am grateful for these experiences, not readily available to most of my contemporaries because of cost; they started a keen life-long love of music, plays, and opera. It was truly a privilege to continue attending these events all the years I lived in the Bay Area. From my earliest years I listened on Saturdays to the broadcast of the Metropolitan Opera from New York. I really got to love those operas but wouldn't admit it to Mother. To disguise my enjoyment I often lay on the floor in front of the radio and worked math problems as I talked teachers into giving me extra math books. I loved the challenge of working in areas I had not studied, trying to figure out the problems, and most often succeeded.

✠

One evening Jack emptied some still smouldering fireplace ashes in the garden close to one of my bedroom windows. I shut the nearby window and opened one on another side of the room but the stench continued. I asked Jack to put the ashes out but he ignored me. I got angry, rushed out, picked up the hose, and doused the smoky coals. I was in a hurry to get back inside; it was cold. I turned carelessly and caught my foot in the hose and fell on the flagstone walk injuring my left wrist. I complained of pain and wanted it bandaged but no one would listen. Mother's first reaction, as usual, was anger. I felt unheard so put on some kind of bandage myself. A few days later, with my wrist still bandaged, I got involved in a baseball game at school. I made a hit of some sort and ran for first base, sliding in like a regular pro. I twisted my leg and the pain prevented putting my weight on that leg. Mother picked me up and took me to the doctor who found a simple fracture but one that would require a cast up to the groin. As the plaster set, the doctor asked about the bandage on my arm and I told him about the injury to my wrist. He x-rayed it, and showed us where it was broken and displaced. I was appalled when he said he needed to give me an anesthetic to fix it. I stayed home for six weeks or more, getting around by hopping, as I couldn't use crutches because of the wrist cast. I had a good time just reading and being lazy.

Over the years I have become aware of how I dismissed physical and psychological pain, put up a good front, belittling the problem, whatever it was. This started when I was small and always wanted to hide any scars, physical or emotional, from Mother's lickings. Injury or surgery each required a rapid recovery; get back to normal as quickly as possible. This life-long pattern of pushing my recovery was evident through the surgeries, illnesses, and diminishments of aging. Thankfully, today I am learning to honour my body in new ways, and to allow it to heal itself at its own, more healthful pace.

Standing before the phonics chart in Miss Young's class was my first introduction to school. I didn't like it. I can still feel myself shaking in my boots if called to the front of the class. Miss Young pointed to the symbols and asked me to sound them out. I don't quite know why, but I didn't get it. Reflecting back I think I just didn't get the point, was embarrassed, and probably didn't even want to try since I could already read. I saw words as a whole almost like a photograph and it made no sense to my brain to break them up. There was no Kindergarten in those days but as I said before, Jack had taught me how to read. Our desks, anchored in rows, had lids that lifted up and inkwells in the corner. It was rather easy for me to lift a lid slightly and read a storybook or do something else besides pay attention to the teacher. I remember getting the lid slammed down on my fingers more than once.

After my good start both Jack and I enrolled at Dunbar the next year; it was a new school which replaced all the one room schools, drawing students from all the nearby towns and the areas between. It was about six miles from home toward Santa Rosa. Classes were small and at first we had three or four grades in one classroom. There were few text books but at least a book for each student in each subject. Dunbar was probably typical of rural schools in those days. We would line up outside, rain or shine, for the Pledge of Allegiance and sometimes a song as well. The teacher led us into our classroom with the usual shoving and pushing as we went in. We had a cloakroom at the back where we hung our coats and put our galoshes. The oiled floors always stank, though they cleaned them each evening with sawdust.

We went back to Sonoma for Third Grade so Milo could get a good start and then returned to Dunbar. In Fifth Grade I had Miss Griffin, an unusually good teacher with an interest in natural history, so I could ask her my questions about nature. She had a large personal library of books that identified flowers, birds, and sea life, beautifully illustrated and containing a wide range of information. Certainly all the pictures were of help in identifying specimens. She soon got me interested in history and always had endless books from her own library for me to read. She also suggested books I could get from the Carnegie Library in Sonoma. Our library visits and home library gave us many hours of reading and a good start in literature. Dad, Mother, Jack, and I were all avid readers and the two younger children eventually caught the same spirit.

Miss Griffin encouraged Jack's and my interest in wild flowers and we gathered them, looked up the Latin names and made a collection of over two hundred flowers we found on our own ranch. The next spring we gathered as many flowers as we could find to put on an exhibit at a science display at the Junior College in Santa Rosa. We took the flowers and bottles up late one afternoon and placed them on tables in a classroom as well as displaying some we had pressed. The next morning we returned and as people came in we discussed our finds with them and answered questions. It was quite an honour to have the display and some people were surprised we knew so much about the flowers. So, with these kinds of projects proposed by our teachers, we did not suffer from the curriculum limitations of a small school. Still, nothing in our early nature study related to how it all came about. There was no mention of the Creator.

In Eighth Grade I was often bored so Miss Griffin arranged for me to spend part of the day helping First graders with reading and playing games with them at recess. I enjoyed my first try at teaching; this early experience stayed with me until my own days as a teacher, twenty-five years later. I went to Sonoma Valley Union High School, a tiny school, for even when I graduated there were only fifty in my class and in those days there were few dropouts. All my years in small schools didn't seem to make it difficult for me in college. Perhaps it was because of my wide reading and opportunities for so many social experiences, whether I liked them or not. God was shaping me for a greater purpose, though I could not see it then.

May 2004. The awe of creation, inspired in me as a child, has been sustained and has grown. Coming to grips with my Creator has helped me know more of the plan of creation. Having spent many years now out in nature I know how much of what I see and find speaks to me. Often when taking pictures of something as simple as a dead leaf, some words come to me and tie my nature observations with my spiritual experiences. This kind of picture-taking speaks of my ever deepening connection with the Creator. Cards or filmstrips were one way of sharing this gift with others. My poetry reflects another kind of interaction with nature; for out in nature, in the silence of all about me, in the simplicity of a leaf or a sound, I know God is touching me...and often, the words of a simple poem come to speak the beauty before my eye.

I SEEK CREATION

I am called to solitude   to quiet
so quiet I can hear the gentle lapping at the water's
        edge
so quiet I hear the water drop from a leaf
the fall of a pine cone sounding the death knell
so quiet I feel presence in my aloneness

Patterns of creation   displayed in all nature
the guiding path
through life's maze; simple
open for all to see and grasp

A whisper in the breeze
  thrusting up of new shoots
  gathering drops of water
  flight of wings
  all about is Your creation.

There You create me
planting seed in my emptiness
new growth sprouts

Filling any void within to capacity
for You, God
are present in me.

BETRAYAL: GROWING INTO TEEN YEARS

It is difficult to recall and to speak about the sexual abuse I suffered at age twelve. It was an experience with powerfully painful ramifications in other areas of my life and the memory has never faded. I now know that family members or friends sexually abused many girls of my generation, and it still goes on to this day. Many have never spoken about being abused, though it certainly has had a negative effect on their lives. As a spiritual director I have often heard stories about abuse and its result in the lives of the victims. Over and over I have also heard that there was no one with whom the child could talk, or there was a broken relationship with a mother. Sometimes they tried to talk it out but no one heard them.

I was one of those girls. One day at the lake we were walking around the shoreline. Four boys, two of them my brothers, stopped and wanted to see what I looked like without my swimsuit. I had no idea as to what they really wanted. They exposed themselves willingly but as I had seen my brothers when they were smaller I wasn't seeing anything new. In my innocence I willingly got down on the ground but as the boys fumbled, each trying to be bigger and better than the other, I got upset. I tried to stop them because of pain and a troubling sense that something just wasn't right; they eventually stopped their attempts to have intercourse. Their giggles and also the fact that they hid the event in the deep bullrushes certainly should have given me a better idea as to what was going on but I was so innocent that I didn't have an inkling as to what was happening. Jack was my idol and I did not understand his actions or his real motives. I certainly had never received any sex education.

I did not say anything to anyone. That same summer another episode with Jack and one of the other boys took place and I sensed something really wasn't right. I stopped them from hurting me further, and just ran away. My brother Jack, who was thirteen at the time, was certainly the instigator of these events and taunted me by saying he would tell Mother and I would get in trouble. He also threatened to tell my friends. Because two boys outside the family had also been involved, this only added to my dilemma. One day, in desperation, I decided to tell Mother. I remember standing in the kitchen—all the bad things always happened there— and trying to tell her what had been going on. I struggled with the language and had a very difficult time expressing myself. I felt maybe the boys' assaults were

81

wrong because of Jack's warning. She was furious with me, very upset, and said that she or Dad would take care of Jack and that I should never do that again.

My lack of understanding and my discussion with Mother caused me to feel I was in the wrong; I felt blamed for the entire event. I couldn't articulate anything accurately. I could only stumble over the words. I remember standing there crying and feeling I was the bad one. I carried that feeling around for a good long time. I did not get an adequate explanation from Mother that day nor in the future though I had unexpressed questions galore. I told Mother not to tell anyone as I had picked up on her blaming me, and felt deeply ashamed. I was totally bewildered because I still didn't understand what really had occurred and still thought Jack was at fault. Certainly my communication with Mother was so difficult I couldn't convey any of it, just accepted the confusion, and went on. I was used to Mother's anger by now, and expected it would always be there.

A few days later Mother and I went to visit one of her friends who had a daughter in my class at school. We were not particularly good friends but I went along to play with her while our mothers had tea. We were walking along the side of the house just below the room where Mother and her friend were talking and I overhead Mother telling her friend about the incident with Jack and the other boys. As soon as I could get my wits about me I started to run so that my friend wouldn't hear any of it. I then went into the house and asked Mother when we were going home. On the way home I told her I had overheard her talking to Gina and that she had said she wouldn't talk to anyone. She insisted that I had misheard but as she was saying this it was just more evident to me that she was telling a lie. I was devastated and cried hysterically nearly all the way home, then ran to my room to be alone in my misery. I did my best to understand what was going on but there was just no way to take it all in. Right at that moment I started another deep life-long pattern, one of not trusting anyone.

My period started within a few months of this event. Mother had not given me any instructions so I was totally unaware of what was going on. Grandma came to my aid. Most girls have uneven periods for a year or more. I remember Mother questioning me one day as to when I had had my last period. When I said it was a couple of months she immediately asked if I had let any boys touch me. I was stunned. I was angry; how could she even think I would let someone come close to me after the episodes with Jack? I never had any real sharing with Mother or anyone else, and it was sometime in my second year at high school before I found a book which gave me some basic facts. Still nowhere to ask questions!

Over the next few years, Jack tried to use the incident to blackmail me and it was difficult to get him to stop. If there was something he wanted me to do for him, and I didn't want to give in, he would quickly say, "I will tell... about you" and there would be an impasse. Gradually I got strong enough to say I would get Dad involved, although I was afraid to do it. I never once considered that Jack would be ashamed by revealing what had gone on between us. Even to this day I don't understand why I hadn't smartened up about his part in it all and used it against him. However, the import of this event took on gigantic proportions because of the lies, the broken trust, and the fact that I had nowhere to get the knowledge or the help I needed in working out the problems as I saw them.

September 2003. Now I realize that Jack probably had not received much sex education himself. He was at the age when he wanted to be a dominant figure, a real man. In many ways he was still a curious kid who wanted to be manly, if you will, a bit before his time. That he repeated his actions toward me when he knew I was ignorant and physically hurt is not excusable. I finally understood that Mother didn't properly or in a timely fashion give me an adequate sex education and she lied to me more than once about what she had said to her friend. Since I did not have a good relationship with Mother I gave extra weight to her untruths and her lack of communication with me. This was, at least on my part, a rift that prevented any openness in our relationship. No trust. No safety.

In my forties I fully realized that any mother would need to talk with a friend about a perplexing problem of this nature. In fact, I know I would do the same. So... this meant I could fully forgive her. Part of my growth work was to forgive myself for not letting it go sooner. It took a longer time for me to forgive myself for judging Mother harshly. I spoke to Mother about the incident a few years before her death, but she had no memory of talking with Gina. For her sake I hope this meant that she had worked it through. It has taken me years to do so.

At no time did I ever attain an easy relationship with my mother. We just never talked about my childhood, she was never comfortable sharing about those early years. It is a shame that we didn't get this emotional impasse cleared up and opened. We both missed out on the richness of knowing and sharing each other's lives.

When Jack and I saw each other as adults we never talked about our life on the ranch. I had buried the abuse incident and the years following so deeply that it never came to my mind to discuss this area. We did not socialize as friends or siblings except in a group situation at Mother and Dad's. No doubt I would have discussed it with Jack at about the time I spoke to Mother, about a year before I entered the monastery, but by then he had died.

The sexual abuse, betrayal, and my constant conflict with Mother became a major struggle in my life. My body had already taken a beating with Mother's lashings. A most important rupture in my growing up took place because of the total change of my relationship with Jack. We were thick as thieves for years. The Jack/Jill combination, enhanced by our isolation at the ranch, was strong. We taught each other many things and I am sure we were closer than most brothers and sisters. I look back at the broken bond with Jack as one of the great sorrows of my life; a loss of a best friend, a person I trusted. A huge loss; I never found a way to remedy the situation before his tragic death.

Jack's betrayal of my body and my affection, and his blackmail attempts, sealed me off in a steel casket. Something died. My Jack had changed, he was no longer a friend, a trusted companion; I was really on my own. Inside, I was insecure and didn't know how I would get to where I was going; making me a loner to be sure.

These events would impact most, if not all, of my life's relationships. Again I told myself that I was a misfit in the family. I often longed to belong, but I had lost the ability to do so. My talents and interests became my only currency for survival. These broken relationships were a monumental obstacle to healthy growing up and seriously impaired my ability to relate with others.

I realize I didn't talk about these episodes with Dad. Somehow I felt I couldn't, even though I had a good relationship with him. It may have been because of my shyness and also my ignorance about all sexual matters. It may also have been that Dad was so busy at the time trying to set up the Guest Ranch that he wasn't around when I could ask questions of him. Anyway it just didn't happen.

Betrayed by Mother and Jack, I felt totally alone at twelve and I could depend only on myself. I learned that I could receive recognition by doing, and began a life-long pattern of working intensely, ignoring my body and my feelings. Moving from activity to activity and being totally immersed in each activity meant not having to face fear or loneliness.

When difficult or painful moments came up in my life I had few skills to work them through to an appropriate conclusion. My practice was to just stuff them inside and escape dealing with them. My response to these childhood events distinctly changed the person God had created. It has taken hours of dialogue with trusted counsellors, and much prayer, but I have banished the shame, hopefully forever. I still have times of struggle with the Lord when memories emerge in my mind and heart. For me, healing has been a lifetime journey and in reality one which has drawn me closer and closer to the Lord. I speak openly of this because I know how very typical stories of this kind of abuse are in women of my generation and those younger than me. I invite any of you abused women to take a straight look at your story, acknowledge it, and work through it to forgive the people concerned. This may allow you to get on with the remainder of your life, not saddened by what happened, but rejoicing that clarity, healing, and love can soften painful memories.

November 8, 2004. I realize I took over my life's direction at the time of the abuse. I became self-directed and did not allow all the pain I had suffered, and was suffering, to interfere with getting broad life experiences. I thought this would be easy but my issues of trust, starting so early with Jack and Mother, certainly got in the way of my making close friends. I like to be with people, but didn't want intimacy; intimacy has always been an issue. Part of it is that I don't know who I am... strong, independent, willing, generous...but with insides lonely and needy. Over the years most of my friendships were at a low level of intimacy or one-sided. I have never had more than one or two friends with whom I can be really me. This is now changing.

✠

A few months later Mother was driving down our road when a car came too fast around the corner and hit us head-on; the impact was severe. I went partially through the windshield, sustaining a cut under my chin, a piece of glass sticking out of my right temple and injury to my back and knees. Dad and others were working on the hill and, hearing the crash, they came running. Dad got me out of the car and I sat on the running board, in shock and scared by the glass poking out from my head. I would not let anyone close, protecting myself from further harm. It seemed like a long time before a car could get past the accident scene to take me to the hospital. There they stitched me up and I was okay except for a headache, poison oak on my face, and painful dark bruises. My knees had hit the dashboard very hard and no doubt this started the knee problems that have been with me ever since. Mother felt guilty as she was the driver but it clearly was not her fault. The accident was terribly traumatic to me; I didn't want to ride down the road any more, and was scared riding with Mother at the wheel.

Mother took me to a specialist in San Francisco about my back and also to a psychologist, perhaps because I wouldn't ride in a car with her, perhaps because it was obvious that I was very unhappy. I remember sitting in a big chair in his office. I felt comfortable with him but was not able to tell the truth about Mother's abuse or the sexual assaults. However, I could and did tell him, when asked, that I did not want to be at home nor go anywhere with my mother. Looking back on those fragments of memory, I probably told him more than enough. He got the point; I was not only unhappy but also abused. The result was that I went to boarding school for Seventh Grade.

There were no boarding schools except those run by Catholic Sisters. I had never seen a Sister except at a distance, in San Francisco. We visited the Ursuline Convent in Santa Rosa and they enrolled me in St. Rose's grammar school, and I boarded with the high school students attending the convent. I slept in the huge dorm that housed about twenty-five, each bed curtained off at night. Our cubicles had a bed, small dresser and a straight chair. There was no light on the stand, so no extra reading for me. St. Rose's School was much harder than Dunbar, but it didn't take me long to catch up and lead the class. And I loved it there.

This was at the height of the Depression so the meals were simple, certainly no seconds at all. A Sister sat at table, served us and taught us manners and directed our conversation. I guess you could call it our class in social graces. And we did act like ladies at all meals. No slouching, no arguing, a far cry from meals at home!

What a contrast from home. I wanted to be away but I also missed the many activities and intriguing finds at the ranch. Sometimes when I had a weekend at home I would just walk away into the hills or across to my favourite spots on the contours, very much a loner. Again, a divided spirit! Of course, I had nothing to do with Jack and as little to do with Mother as possible.

I thought my teacher, Sister Columba, was ancient, but she was only in her mid-twenties. Her ears and eyes were always busy and we got away with nothing. Mother told me, as did Sister Columba, that I was to sit in the back and read a storybook during religion class. As I said, I was contrary and whenever someone would say, "You can't" or "Don't do" then I did. I would sit with a book in front of my face but would keep my ears wide open. I began to get a smattering of religious facts but really couldn't relate them to anything for a long time.

The year at the Ursuline Convent was the first time I learned anything positive about God. My classmates spoke of God as someone you could pray to if you needed something. Also as someone you could thank. Like more of a real person. I was still confused but their talk of God sparked my interest. I don't think our family even had a Bible when I was small, or at least I am not aware of one; that is a bit strange as we had books on everything. At the convent I took study hall in the evening with the older girls, so I went to the library and got books about spiritual things. I read all the lives of the saints I could get. I remember that I wanted to talk with the Curé of Ars after I read his story. He came across as someone anyone could talk to and I needed someone like that to help me. Over fifty years later I went out of my way to attend Sunday mass in his church in France. It was a tiny church on the main street of a small village; the interior and the confessional just as they were in the Curé's day.

My curiosity increased and when I began to study the Baltimore Catechism I hid it behind a geography book. It didn't take me too long to catch up enough to understand what the religion class was studying in school. Gradually, I just took part and sometime toward the end of the year would even answer Father Rater's questions; I am sure he did not know I was not a Catholic.

As I said, I had a poor understanding of God and wanted to know more about the church that I heard about in the classroom. I started to go to mass each morning, sitting in the back pew close to the hall entrance. As soon as kneeling started I would pass out— and I would have no idea why—and one of the Sisters would get me off the floor. Gradually I got used to the kneeling and went daily although, of course, not to communion. During October and later in May I regularly took part in the evening Rosary. My body was there but I hadn't the slightest understanding about how one prayed the Rosary. I could say the prayers and thought that was all there was to it.

April 2003. It has been difficult for me to feel that I was worthy of love, that God loved me first and loves me always. I am now in my eighties and at times I still struggle with this concept. I did not have any sense of what God's unconditional love was all about but now I look forward to seeing God face to face.

Through all my reading about the church and the saints I decided that Catholicism was the true religion and it appealed to me. I had heard and verified in my reading that the church founded by Christ's early followers is the Catholic Church and those who protested its rules in some way founded all other Christian churches. Thus, to me as a child I wanted the real church and eventually it became mine. Thankfully, I have now broadened my concept of church.

Throughout the school year I continued gathering religious teachings and at Easter, when the Episcopalians had confirmation, I was on the list against my wishes. I met with the bishop, the rector and someone else and remember talking to them about why I should become a Catholic instead of an Episcopalian. I thought I had my answers down pat but it didn't work; I was on the confirmation list. I always said it didn't take as my veil slipped off and I made no effort to put it back on properly. I did continue to attend that church through high school, because I was made to do so, but it didn't do anything for me. I just sat there. I finished the Seventh Grade at the convent and then returned to Dunbar, but obviously the year of being touched by God stuck with me through the next years until I left home for college at Stanford.

I took piano from Miss Dresel from about the time I was six. I wasn't any good, hated it, but did practice and at least managed to get good at scales. I had switched to violin and continued with my lessons while at the convent. They had practice rooms and I did not like one of the Sisters who kept checking up on me. I tried to defy her by putting on a mute and also stuffing a hankie under the bridge. She would come to the door and jerk it open to see what I was doing. I was always practicing but I soon got the point that she had to hear me. In high school I played with the orchestra.

✠

In 1934 Dad opened a stable and bought a few more horses to add to his already good string. There were always people who enjoyed riding on the twenty-five miles of trails on the mountainside. They were easy trails, going into a variety of woodlands and meadows with good views of the beautiful valley. The people went out in small groups with a guide so even novice riders felt safe. I don't know much about how this came about but eventually people who came from a distance, like from San Francisco, wanted to stay over. We built some cabins and also refurbished some of the rooms that Jack London had used years before as guest rooms. Dining facilities, including the kitchen, were improved and in 1935 the Jack London Guest Ranch opened, being able to handle up to twenty five people. This flourished for many years, until Dad gave it up some years after the end of WWII.

Dad was fun to be with and we talked about the ranch goings on and the people there as we drove to Santa Rosa in the pickup. No one else wanted to shop with him because Dad limited his shopping to the needs of the ranch and did not go window or clothes shopping. I learned how to purchase vegetables, about cuts of meat, serving sizes, and what to buy and how much according to the size of the group of visitors. When anything new came up Dad would explain or let me ask my own questions of the butcher or others serving us. I also worked on the menus. We shopped for anything needed for the rooms and for cleaning supplies as well.

As I got more experienced I went off on my own to do the shopping if Dad was busy with other things; I got my license on my fourteenth birthday and was able to go anywhere on my own. There was not much traffic in those days and I was good at changing a tire because there were no gas stations except in towns; I even got good at putting a patch on the inner tube. Many of these experiences with the guest house helped me when I began to run a retreat house in Oregon and later in Canada. True, Dad was no help with my interactions with Mother and we didn't discuss her. Even though I saw little of him as an adult I always felt a close connection to him until his death in 1974.

When I was fifteen one of our neighbors, Pete Narvaez, who worked in the laboratory at Eldridge, the Sonoma State Hospital, asked me if I would like to do volunteer work in the lab on Saturdays mornings. Not even knowing what it was about, I said yes. This institution was home to five thousand residents who were handicapped by mental retardation or birth defects. Mother was against my working there, saying I was too young. Pete had just hired a young woman, about twenty-one, who had recently finished her training as a bacteriologist. Everything about the lab work was new to me; I learned to use a microscope and to take precise measurements. Laboratory work really caught me up in a new direction. As a result of this contact Marilla and I became good friends and went riding together. Marilla married during WWII and went to live in Berkeley; we continued as friends until she was in her seventies and moved to Utah and lost contact.

For many years when we were on the ferry to San Francisco we would watch the building of the Golden Gate Bridge. On opening day, May 27, 1937, Dad, Grandma Ranker and all of us children drove to Sausalito, took the ferry to San Francisco, parked our car and then walked over to Sausalito, nearly a mile, and back to San Francisco. It was a memorable occasion for us all as well as the thousands of others who made the walk that day. It was blustery and Grandma and I had to hold our skirts whenever we crossed an expansion joint, otherwise people would have seen our underwear. Another "first day event" was our trip over the Bay Bridge that is over eight miles long and in part anchored at Yerba Buena Island. On opening day in November 1936, Dad drove from the San Francisco side, taking three hours to cross; then he whipped across a couple of lanes and we went on the lower deck, not yet used for trucks and it took only about twenty minutes to cross and we were off for home.

I graduated at the top of my tiny class from Dunbar and gave a speech about the Golden Gate Bridge that we had walked across about two weeks earlier. I went to Sonoma High School that fall, where Miss Godward immediately picked me out as a good math student. She gave me a steady supply of alternate texts and even

95

let me take them home. This firmly planted my love of math. At the end of geometry class we had a Columbia Research Examination and I had a perfect score. Columbia thought it was a fluke but another test proved I was especially good at geometry. Miss Godward and I clicked. Her guidance of me as a student demanded that I work at my growing edge in all subjects and strive for excellence. Her influence gave me confidence to tackle any subject; I was the first girl to take Mechanical Drawing, even over the opposition of the male teacher, who only wanted to teach boys so they could swear whenever they wanted.

Dad had bought me a fine 35mm Leica camera when he was in Germany, to replace my box Kodak that I had used for several years. Of course, I had only black and white film so I did quite a bit of work in the darkroom, including sneaking a kiss from one of the boys. Our education was more personalized than in larger schools and thus helped us succeed as we went on to further education. Some of us started college in the fall of 1941 but later interrupted our college education because of war service. The G.I. Bill after the war enabled many other classmates to complete college and enter professions.

Another wonderful event, repeated many, many times, was attendance at the World's Fair on Treasure Island, an offset of Yerba Buena Island, the middle anchor for the Bay Bridge. To get to Treasure Island one turned off half way to Oakland. It was a beautiful setting with a view all around the Bay. We went from school on opening day and some Saturdays, paying a transportation charge of twenty-five cents and the same for entrance. As we went often, we saw all the foreign exhibits and many of the concerts and shows. On the last day, as the fair was closing, Carrie Jacobs Bond, a noted American composer, sang her composition "The End of a Perfect Day". She was about eighty-two at the time and it made a life-long impression on me. It was the end of an era, for already the war had started in Europe; who knew what the coming months and years would bring? I certainly didn't. So I am grateful that my early years and teens too gave me such a broad base of social events which would help me to be comfortable with whatever the future might bring.

> April 2003. When I was eighty some of the lay people here in Nanaimo had an event for me entitled Memorable Moments with Jill. As a way of tying my life together, and as a special treat, Sister Mary Ann sang "The End of a Perfect Day" for me, bringing a few tears to my eyes.

In 1938 our family met Laura and Oliver Grant from San Francisco. Laura was acting as a local hostess for the Latin American Consular Corps. The Grants lived on the steepest part of Hyde Street in a large, gracious apartment with spectacular views out across to the Golden Gate and Marin. One time Mrs. Grant, whom I was loath to call Laura as she was about sixty, asked me to help her serve at a cocktail party. My cousin Roslyn and I both responded and over the next couple of years, often went down to help at such an event.

Interaction with such a group of international figures offered me a unique chance to broaden my life experiences. Meeting these people, socially, made me more comfortable when I encountered other social and educational situations later in life. While I never liked to be in large groups, I could do so and knew the manners required for such events.

Years later, when San Francisco was the site for the first meetings of the United Nations, one of the Consuls asked me if I would like to attend a session with him. I was home for a short leave from the Army so off I went in my Sergeant's suit. It was an extraordinary event for me and I was thankful for the opportunity. They had earphones to hear the translations, allowing everyone to understand the speaker. I was sorry that I couldn't go again as one could really sense history being made; I had to get back to Florida.

✠

The onset of a serious illness which continued to affect me my whole life came soon after my sixteenth birthday. It was the forerunner of several more heartaches and losses before I was twenty. It was a very long time ago; however the pain, grief, emotional baggage, and memories are still present in the dark recesses of my mind. The insults to my body are less powerful because of healing but the evidence is still there.

The day after school closed in early June 1939, I woke with a terrible pain, a cramping pain severe enough to make me double over trying to protect myself from the next onslaught. Steeling myself, I got to the breakfast table to find that Mother had fallen and broken her leg the night before. So I straightened up, put on a good face, and went to see her. She was quite uncomfortable lying with her foot in a basket to protect it from the weight of blankets on her toes. She said she was just going to stay in bed and didn't want breakfast.

I thought my pain would let up, but it didn't, so somehow I drove the five miles to the lab where my friend Pete took a blood count. It didn't seem indicative of appendicitis so I drove back home, hoping that the pain was just a menstrual pain or some kind of fluke. Maybe it was just my imagination. But it wouldn't stop and I doubled up in agony, trying to will the pain away. Finally, I had to admit that something was wrong and Dad drove me to the doctor in Sonoma.

After a careful examination Dr. Andrews said I had a very large ovarian cyst that needed immediate surgery but I needed to see a specialist. Dad and I talked it over and the next thing I knew we were on the way to Oakland, some fifty miles distant, to see my Uncle Emery, my mother's brother, who was a general surgeon. I hardly knew him because he had been in the Chicago area for medical school and specialty education. He had only recently opened his office in Oakland. When we arrived he examined me and rushed me into the hospital for immediate surgery though it was late afternoon. We walked across the street to the hospital and they admitted me.

I tried to be strong and upbeat for Dad. Inside I was frightened nearly to death. I didn't know what an ovarian cyst was, and had only the vaguest idea about what the surgical procedure was going to be. They told me the bare minimum and questions didn't seem appropriate. It didn't take long to get me ready for surgery; I was to have a spinal anesthetic as they thought it would be easiest on me. I remember I sat up straight and they put a needle in my spine, I felt a horrible, sudden, sharp pain but I held as still as I could. Then they took me into the operating room.

I must have been given some kind of sedation, but know that my fear of what was going to happen overcame many of its effects. I remember lying there and hearing the other surgeon and my uncle discussing what they were going to do. When they opened me up they saw the cyst was huge, and I remember they had difficulty getting it out. They spoke about how serious it was, "touch and go" was their comment. This frightened me more, but being Jill, I added to my own fear because I looked up at the lamp overhead. This acted as a mirror so I could see just what they were doing. The instruments all about fascinated me. I could see the surgeon's hands moving and saw the cyst as they got it out, but they nicked it on the way out and it began to collapse.

Enough! The doctors said something about serious difficulties so I closed my eyes and decided to pray. I wasn't certain about how to do that, not even what to say. Being still afraid of God I wasn't sure who I could speak to. So, I reached back to my days at the Ursuline convent. I tried to remember one of the prayers we said when we lined up in the hall for the Rosary, but they were gone from my mind; I couldn't remember even a Hail Mary. I just talked with the Blessed Mother, asking her to be with me, to help so that I could live, for part of my fear was that something was going wrong and

I might die and I wasn't ready for that. I have no idea how long I pleaded, sincerely pleaded with her to intervene and made a vow, a deep heart-felt promise that if I recovered I would look into how to become a Catholic. I had to become a Catholic, for the study and spiritual insights from the convent had already convinced me that Catholicism was the one true faith. This much I believed, but of course it was an intellectual belief and of little help to me at such a time of distress.

I knew that a vow made to God had to be kept but I also knew I would have to wait until I was on my own. I did not conceive of not following through. Perhaps some of this was my desperate need for someone to be close at a time of serious struggle. In this sense, God was responding to my need and call, though I really didn't feel anything except scared.

I had a long two-week stay in the hospital and a fast recovery, not knowing what, if any, repercussions would come from losing my entire right ovary. If anyone brought up the subject of my surgery, I shrugged it off by saying "Just nothing", really meaning, "I don't need you". I didn't or couldn't explain what was going on within me.

February 2003. What a liar I was! I didn't know anything else to say; after all I was a strong competent sixteen-year-old and life was to be lived full steam ahead. My feelings, and there were many—mostly fear about what part I was missing—were ignored or were so uncomfortable that I just packed them away in my stuffing bag. I couldn't discuss it with anyone for I didn't know

101

anyone who knew more than I did and neither Mother nor Grandmother brought up the topic for discussion or solicited questions that would be helpful.

I lost some of myself at the time, wasn't quite sure what this loss would mean, and I didn't understand; I was unable to speak about my personal needs. This only kept me more distant from people and more independent than ever. Once more I had no support, nurturing, or comfort, yet some would certainly have been helpful to my recovery.

I know that I wondered if the sexual abuse had in any way contributed to the ovarian cyst. I had no one to ask. I just wasn't able to take it up even with Dr. Andrews, so again I just felt guilty and confused. I don't know where I got the courage but life just had to be lived and as soon as possible I returned to working for Dad at the ranch, or in the lab. I got into diverse activities there and found it interesting to measure out ingredients to make media, learning to pipette solutions, including one day getting some gentian blue into my mouth. Pete had to wash it out with acid alcohol so there would be no evidence for Mother to see. I had a mighty sore mouth for some days but it was worth it because if Mother had known I would have had to quit. I think my interest in biological sciences increased because of my experiences at the lab. Consequently, when I went off to college I entered as a pre-med student.

I graduated at the top of my class in high school and Stanford accepted me, starting in the fall of 1941.

Mother had a need for show and this was evident at my high school graduation. I had been very ill for some weeks with a kidney infection and a temperature of 103 degrees. The doctor had actually advised that I not attend graduation even though I was Valedictorian. Mother insisted that I go. Again, I felt no caring so I went unprepared and had a terrible time getting up from my chair to receive the California Scholarship Federation Life Award and to give my speech. I barely got out of there and went directly to the car and then home.

Mother was angry with me because I did not stay and greet people; it was rude, she said, but I had been in bed off and on for over six weeks. There were no drugs for most of the illness; only in the last stage did I get some Sulfa, which had just come on the market. The stress of graduation was horrendous because of the fear of needing a bathroom in the middle of the ceremony, as well as the constant pain. My speech was not up to par because of little preparation. As I look back I realize it was not at all the joyful event it should have been, it was one filled with disappointment and suffering.

October 2004. Mother was never the mom or the one I sought out when I was a child at home. I'm sorry because I really never knew her well. It wasn't to be. On occasion I have been jealous of other mother-daughter relationships. I accept Mother more fully now as I understand the conditions under which she lived and raised her children. As I work on my story I realize that as she

103

got older and pressure was less she was no doubt a different woman. She always had many friends and as we left the nest she and Dad entertained frequently, and were both well loved and respected in the community. As I said, I long ago forgave her for her part in my own mixed up early start in life and some of the incidents that left long, ugly scars. However, we never had a good understanding of each other. Criticism started too early and I no doubt anticipated its presence and responded rather automatically. Neither of us was able to bridge the gap. Yet I know that Mother was my parent, selected for a good reason, and I am the woman I now am because of her standing against and with me, early on. I accept this as a blessing for indeed, all troubles aside, I wouldn't want to re-do my life again. Pain and all blessings say my life was and is a good one and one of which I can be proud. My life will never be long enough to allow me to do all the creative things I still have in mind, or to complete the spiritual growth still facing me.

August 14, 2004. (On this date I went to a business meeting for the ranch and these are excerpts from my journal.)

I may well have seen the ranch for the last time. My head says this makes sense but again, my heart is not there. I think my work with my life story these past months has increased my awareness of what the ranch really means to me. It has been a source of hell and a source of joy and of responsibility. I didn't get a chance to go out by myself into some of my favourite spots, but the trip to the Wolf House in a golf cart took me back many years. As we passed the old orchard, lots of memories returned; Jack and I used to pick Muscat grapes, figs, and apples if we wandered over there in late summer. At the Wolf House we walked up to one of the lookout spots but couldn't go inside; it was not safe. It brought back memories of playing hide and seek there as a child. We did not go to London's grave, which is nearby; it is also the resting place of Charmian, Grandmother Shepard and my parents; I just couldn't walk up that hill, it was too steep for me.

Later, Milo drove us around the vineyard and while general conversation was going on I recalled some of the incidents that took place at various spots as I looked across at buildings or hills, now changed by time and planting. The pink house is gone, but there were signs that the creek which fed the snake hole still ran in winter. I remembered as if it were yesterday, how Jack and I used to spend time in the old barns and treat others to a ride in the manure dumper.

It is good that the State is putting all the buildings into good repair. It is a beautiful ranch and I am glad that now most of it belongs to the park so no houses or roads will ruin its natural beauty. The contours of my childhood, planted in grapes, are just now turning, being about a month from harvest. A good crop this year! It is a good idea for the future generation to make the best use of

105

the inheritance they will receive by learning to work together now. This means hands off for all of us in my generation. All this makes sense, but deep within I know that it is hard for me to give up control, to acknowledge this is another area of loss, and another way of saying, "You are over the hill, and get on with it". I don't like this; it hurts to be on the back burner, even if I myself am one of the ones putting me there. Somehow, I need to more fully face the diminishment and accept it as my own choice, made when I really looked at the goings on in my generation.

I really wish I could just cry, but again that was one of the things that became so apparent to me as I revisited the ranch. I was in total charge, but not in control, of myself when I was there as a child. I learned not to cry there, and for good reason I thought, but realize that the effects impact me still. I need to cry about the loss, all the kinds of loss and at the same time to know that my God-given strength to go forward, forging ahead into life, has made me a strong and independent woman who in her way did accomplish things for others. I know I can't have it both ways. My life patterns, often involving too much work, seemingly stop me from being softer and more able to express my needs for closeness and care, and to accept the love offered to me. Change is coming, slow, but sure.

On My Own

When I was at Stanford I certainly was not one of the top students, though I did enjoy the privilege of being in honours classes in English, Humanities, and Biology. We had special teachers, assignments, and small groups, which all suited me very well. At that time social life on weekends consisted of going out to dinner and dancing in San Francisco, or at least dancing at the major hotels. I often went, in a long dress, to the Palace, the Mark Hopkins, Sir Francis Drake, and St. Francis, for of course all the best bands played at these hotels. We would choose our hotel depending on who was playing and we danced to Sammy Kay, Glen Miller, Benny Goodman and many more name bands. The boys always had to pay, but there were plenty of fellows with money. Sometimes I was the driver back to school, as I never took a drink. In those days Stanford was just an hour away if I stepped on it. Life was going well, except for a bit of shyness. Though a small town girl I was quite comfortable as a student in a large University on my own; making my own decisions, and setting my directions gave me new life. I became good at masking any discomfort. I had friends, but no confidants.

One day, when I was home from college and driving to Santa Rosa from the ranch, I decided to go to the Ursuline convent and see Sister Columba, my Seventh Grade teacher. I was a bit scared as I went to the door and rang the bell. Sister had gone; she was teaching in San Francisco so I took her phone number and, on my way back to college, stopped and called her. She asked me to come to the school and I did. It had been six years since I had seen her. I told her of my surgery and the vow I made that day; as always it was difficult to speak about my deep feelings. Head stuff was all I could speak about, but my heart was full of a longing to know more about God and to know I was in the right place, if I was going to worship at all. I was quite black and white in my beliefs. I knew I had vowed to become a Catholic and as I did survive that surgery, I needed to take the next step. We talked about seeing a priest and then taking his advice. Sister made some statement to the effect that I would never pursue it; this only acted as a challenge.

February 2, 2003. The God thread was never broken, perhaps only hanging on with half a strand, but as I reflect back I am able to see how God continued to call me to life, to give my life direction and support. This is so obvious since it was only within a few months of being away at

108

Stanford that I decided to seek God for myself, knowing I was free to do as God called. I am sure some of the change, perhaps loneliness in college life and responsibilities suggested to me a need for spiritual support. I don't know what it was at this time, but something reminded me of my vow. On the way back to Stanford I stopped in Palo Alto, took a cab to the Catholic Church and met the priest, who invited me to return the next day for instructions. And I did. I had no one for a sponsor but he knew one of the girls in my dorm and she became my godmother. I became a Catholic the Tuesday before Ash Wednesday in 1942, at St. Thomas Aquinas Catholic Church. I will never forget, I had to make a general confession and my friend drove me round and round the block so I could get enough courage to go in. The priest met me by appointment and the next day I received my first Holy Communion. I belonged and began to read and study more about my new faith. It was still the time when most homilies were about all of our shortcomings; there was no feeling of a loving God.

I was a very regular churchgoer and gave up smoking each Lent. I stopped smoking at midnight on Saturday and resumed it again on Sunday at midnight. My will was strong but my understanding of Lent was obviously not very deep. I can't remember how I told my family, but when Mother found out about my conversion she was very angry. I did not go home for three months. Except for our household help, Mother probably knew only two or three Catholics. I did not know Aunt Kate Hill was a Catholic for when we visited the beach with her she never spoke of going to church, and she certainly ate hot dogs on Fridays. The only Catholics I knew were Pete Narvaez, and Mrs. Barsi and her family. Even after I became a Benedictine Sister, Mother still harboured some resentment.

November 2004. From age eighteen until the time I began to make retreats at about age twenty-nine, all I gathered in was head stuff. I was faithful in attending Mass all those years. Over many years, even into my marriage, when times started to get hard for me I would go to Sunday Benediction. Week after week I would just be there in the quiet of exposition before the actual service. Something kept on drawing me there but I didn't really understand it. Perhaps it was a way to escape, just to have some time to myself. Looking back now though, I know that I did feel a sense of presence that was somehow comforting and something I desperately needed.

NOW

Yesterday is past, tomorrow not yet here
reality... the present moment.
life is gift... like the sun rising,
pursuing its path across the sky, setting, rising again
    and again.

True living is not seeing the obvious, the usua
but that which my mind's eye, my soul, knows is
    best for me.
Insight comes from a source beyond my being
there is no end to the life force, strength showered ·
    upon me.

I need to become silent, still, listen
become so surrendered
only God's word speaks
fullness, wholeness, presence bring re-creation
yesterday's color
forms the present moment.

Drawn to authenticity
springing from roots of times past
life is a prayer
I open myself to the creation going on within me
become more truly and uniquely self
Mystery, presence   unrevealed   breathed into me.

I give praise
seek the wholeness
the oneness of God's presence
now   today   and forever

That winter while at Stanford I was again bothered by
pain in my side, similar to the pain I had had at age
sixteen, but now it was on the left side. It proved to
be a cyst which needed surgery but I went on to finish
the quarter, and then took a leave. At this surgery they
removed half of the ovary and tightened the pedicle
which had apparently been twisting and causing the
trouble. More hell, yet I was beginning to understand
my anatomy. No emotional support; still no one I felt
I could talk with about my situation.

After three weeks—far too short a time, according
to the doctor—I went back to my normal life, stuffing fears, anxieties, and my questions. In spite of the
fact that I was doing well in school I chose not to go
back until the next term. I got a room in a guest house
near St. Brigit's church and got my first paying job at
the Navy Medical Supply Depot in San Francisco. I
lost myself in my work, my way of handling the turmoil inside. Apparently, I came across as particularly
competent, or sold them on my talents, as the job in
Navy supply was demanding, intricate and also under
deep wraps because of secrecy during wartime. My office was the one that routed the antibiotics, serums,
and perishables to the ships in the Pacific. I had to be
sure that we could deliver the packages to the various

ships, so a lot of my work was highly classified. Getting the various needed items, seeing them packaged appropriately and getting them to my office for shipping was a demanding job. Our office was on the waterfront near the ferry building, and secrecy demanded I go in a car by myself when I went to Headquarters; even an Admiral couldn't ride with me. I guess it was good not to know just how much secrecy was involved or I probably would have been afraid.

Having missed the spring quarter at Stanford due to the surgery, I went back in summer to complete the year, and then transferred to the University of California at Berkeley. When I first went to Stanford I met Harry on a blind date and began to fall in love. We spent many an afternoon and evening together. He was a senior that fall when I had transferred to Cal. The Saturday night after the Cal-Stanford football game we went with a group of our friends to Pebble Beach. It was a tradition, which I think probably is still carried out, that the well-to-do students would go to the Del Monte Lodge at Pebble Beach for dinner, dancing and to stay overnight. It was a fun night, a good dinner, and dancing. We had planned to go to Mass at the Monterey Mission. The girls decided we would not change but would go in our evening clothes, also part of the tradition. When I got down to the desk to meet Harry he was not there; he had left me a note saying he was sorry but he couldn't seriously date a Catholic and the car keys were there for me to take those who wanted to go, to church. I was devastated but kept it to myself until we could talk. Later that day Harry said that since I was a Catholic only a short time he wanted

113

me to give it up and become a Presbyterian. I just could not believe such an arbitrary attitude on his part so we ultimately broke up. I continued with my classes at Cal, finishing the fall semester.

Of course, again Mother was not happy with me but I refused to discuss it with her. This was the first time I really had to choose between my faith and another way of life, even for a man I thought I loved. I know that the whole of my conversion came from deep within and it was not something I would ever want to change. Thankfully, God has continued to bless my journey with Catholicism throughout my entire life. Trials and tribulations plagued me at various times in my life; opportunities for spiritual growth were equally present, especially following the war years, and continue to this day. Always, it seems as if the right input, retreat experience, lecture or spiritual director was put into my path just when I most needed it.

Within a few months I noticed more and more pain around the time of my period and often had a catch in my side so strong it made it difficult to stand straight. It continued to get worse so I consulted a Dr. Alice Maxwell, a wonderful woman surgeon, head of the GYN dept at UC San Francisco Medical School. Dr. Maxwell treated me for some months, hoping that things would quiet down, but finally said my condition demanded surgery and that she would do whatever she could to preserve my ability to have children. I remember her coming to visit me the evening after the surgery and telling me things went well and she would talk to me the next day. She had on evening clothes as she was going to the opera but just wanted to personally reassure me. Little did either of us guess that one of the residents would come in and say, "She really cleaned you out". Shocked by her statement I took charge of the conversation saying sharply that Dr. Maxwell would discuss it with me tomorrow, and she stopped talking right then.

This was anguish for I was not only just back from the surgery but also upset because I did not know of the long-term effects of the surgery. The next day Dr. Maxwell came in and she explained there was no possibility of my ever having children. I told her about the incident with the resident and she was very angry saying it was inappropriate and she would speak to her. Though Dr. Maxwell was kind and good I wasn't able to share my fears, or my pent up feelings with her; I just stuffed them, put on a good mask, and went on with life. Today there would be psychological help available for anyone going through this kind of surgery. Keeping it all to myself was a serious mistake, but no one read my hidden need. I went through menopause instantly, as one does when they remove all ovarian tissue. Such a surgical shock is no simple process for anyone and at twenty, I assure you it was terrible. You can imagine my embarrassment at suddenly having unexplained flashes and flushes show up at the most inopportune times. It was not possible to give me any hormone replacement because of the pathology found, so these flashes went on for months.

After my recovery from this last surgery I rarely went to the ranch. My home was a room in a guest house in San Francisco which was quiet. I spent countless evening hours alone, was quite lonely and plagued with questions as to what I would do in the future. With the war on I did not want to return to college, so I applied for and immediately got a job at the U.S. Army Supply Depot in Oakland. It was only a short ride on the train across the bridge and I got off at the first stop and walked to the Medical Supply Depot. I worked in a huge warehouse where I picked up and coded shipments of supplies as requested by some of the smaller Army units.

This time was hard for me. I read a lot, tried to pray, but nothing seemed to affect my loneliness or help in sorting out my future direction. Being alone and being lonely are not the same. I remember spending much of my extra time in St. Bridgit's Church, which was just two blocks from my rooming house. It became a safe haven for me. Sometimes on the way home I stopped at a drug store and played some pinball machines. It was a way to fill in time. I unexpectedly became quite good at it, but it was only a distraction and a useless skill that cost a dime a game so I decided it was too expensive. It cost almost as much as a pack of cigarettes and smoking was by now a fully developed habit.

I had acquired the head knowledge that answered some questions but not the ones which constantly came to my mind. For years I was in denial without really knowing it. Over the years, with good help and much understanding, I have come to realize that I am indeed a whole woman, even with a few parts missing. The tragedy of this kind of surgery is that it left me without the appropriate hormones until I was thirty-seven, by which time my heart was rather seriously damaged and I had a lot of other medical problems.

God is good though, and insightful counselling, along with new medical and drug discoveries, have helped to lessen some of the damage as I have aged.

January 2003. The surgery issues, the starkly real physical changes as well as the emotional impact, called for a radical adjustment in my future outlook on life as a woman; I never found anyone safe for me to talk it over with until I was at least at mid-life. It was hard, nearly impossible for me to get in touch with my real feelings. Honesty would call me to say that I was ashamed and felt half a woman with the essential parts gone but it is also true that I only survived by not thinking, not allowing myself to feel certain kinds of things.

There is no doubt in my mind that I carried some of these erroneous feelings into my decision to marry and then throughout my entire married life. I was not consciously aware of the impact of all this surgery, but my closed off emotional response had a negative impact on my marriage and relationship with my husband, Hank.

PRAYER

My prayer opens   exposes me to Your penetrating
    glance,
You know my unspoken need
clay in your hands… mold me

You free me to grow
to become a person of prayer
I tread an obscure path,
your companionship sustains

Be prayer
teach me to give thanks   praise   adore
to ask forgiveness.

Prayer demands change   risk taking
Prayer faces me to the truth of where I am
who I am

Prayer is You, O God
words of comfort
Prayer is expecting   waiting to be touched.

Open me to Your presence,
give me patience to hear Your word
alone with You
everywhere   forever

Army Marriage

When the war in Europe started in 1939 I was more than usually interested in the news because of our many contacts with family friends in England and Europe. We got the weekly magazine *Illustrated London News* from England, and reading the news it contained made it obvious that one day we would be directly involved in the war. My college years had been a time of ups and downs, with my faith and also my health. The war was bringing change everywhere. Pearl Harbor had a tremendous impact on those in my generation. Nearly all the men I knew were off to war, like it or not. I was always patriotic; I think some of this came from my association with Grandmother Shepard and her continual support of those who served their country in war. I thought of joining the armed forces, as they were asking for women for non-combat duty. I tried to enter the Navy but didn't pass the physical because of

119

my recent surgery so I entered the WAC in the fall of 1943. I had told Dad I wanted to enlist so he signed for me. Mother was aghast. She felt I was far too young to start such a life. Mother was afraid of the company I would keep, a kind of snobbishness for sure.

January 2004. The Fall of 1943 was a difficult time for me. As I look back I picture myself as a lonely woman, working and coming back each afternoon to a quiet evening with my nose in a book. Still caught in the aftermath of the surgery, the impact this would have on all my life; it would never go away! Do not feel! I trusted no one. I think I was afraid to let reality touch me or to fully acknowledge it. I was blind to my denial; my coping skills were immature. Just grin and bear it. I did not ask questions of myself as to what I wanted or could do with the future. It was impossible for me to ask the "what if" questions. It was hell, as I look back on this time.

My only real skill was "to do" and this I did by running headlong into military service; to get away from myself and my family, as if I could. I went to Des Moines, Iowa for basic training. It was hard stuff but it went quite well. We had mental tests, shots and some basic training in marching. In Iowa they surely have dusty sunsets with a myriad of changing colours. I remember how beautiful it was standing out on the parade ground when the flag was brought down in the evening, which also signalled that the end of a stressful day was near at hand, just dinner and bed. I was always ready for both.

After Basic my first assignment was to Advanced Administration School at Conway, Arkansas, where a small college became a centre for the training of administrators for both army and navy personnel. I was there for some months, including my first Christmas away from home. On Christmas Eve we walked a mile to the parish church for midnight Mass. Mass opened with all the children walking in procession around the church with the littlest one carrying the Baby Jesus as carols filled the church. Family groups contributed to the warmth of the celebration. It was snowing hard when we walked down but most of us were unaware of how fast the snow could pile up. What a surprise as we left church to find snow nearly a foot deep. We all had warm overcoats and boots, thank goodness. We trudged back through the snow, made hot chocolate, and ate more of the goodies sent by Grandma and Mother.

I trained as an Administrative Secretary but somehow, perhaps a bit deliberately, I never got beyond twenty-five words per minute in typing, though I otherwise topped the class. Actually, I cheated, as did several others, not wanting to be stuck as a secretary. Grits and navy beans for breakfast, typical southern dishes, got a good laugh from all of us from the West.

My assignment was to the hospital in Wilmington, North Carolina but when I arrived, there was no suitable job for me. So I applied for my first three-day pass and went off to New York to visit friends. I knew little about transportation and how crowded everything was but I soon found out, as I had to sit on my suitcase from North Carolina to Washington D.C. It was about a four-hour trip and I was so tired that I got off in Washington, rented a bathroom, took a shower, changed clothes and went to get a bite to eat before the next train to New York. I sat at a counter next to someone who started to get over-friendly. Another Sergeant sat down right next to me and acted as if he knew me, so the other man stopped annoying me. This was my first introduction to my husband, Hank, for he was that Sergeant. Hank was determined to save me from attention I obviously didn't want. He was quiet about how he did it but his strength and apparent interaction with me scared the other man off. My eyes took in a short slight man with a quick eye for details, for he had seen my distress, and his immediate conversation was on a topic which was of interest to me. In no time we were talking about where we were from, where we were going to, and noting that we shared many interests in common. We were both stationed in North Carolina, he at Fort Bragg and I at Wilmington. I had never set eyes on him before, but we talked so much we both missed our trains.

Hank was a non-com in the Supply Corps. He explained that he was a Sergeant because he didn't want to be cannon fodder as an officer in the Infantry, though he was well qualified for a commission. Hank had been teaching English at Villanova, a Catholic College in Pennsylvania, before his induction. He had always gone to Catholic schools, graduating from St. Joseph's College in Philadelphia and then attending Villanova, where he took his Masters degree in English; he planned to get his doctorate after the war and teach at a college. We talked about all kinds of things that interested us

122

and decided to meet soon in North Carolina. Hank had already promised to spend his short leave with his parents in Clementon, N.J., so he couldn't go to New York with me.

I went on to New York; saw friends and Sister Columba, who was taking some advanced work in New Rochelle, N.Y. I did quite a bit of sightseeing, avidly reading the tourist guides from the hotel and thus enjoyed my first visit to New York City. One of my friends and I took a boat around the harbour but we were not allowed to climb up inside the Statue of Liberty. We did our own tour on buses and the streetcars clear to the Bowery, where we walked a bit. The overview of New York from the top of the Empire State building, and the strong wind were both breathtaking.

Thinking back on this event, now I realize I was again the strong, independent gal because I took off totally alone on this trip to New York. True, I had a couple of people to see, but this was my first stay in a large hotel, completely alone in this great city. Like all who visit there I found it exciting. San Francisco is a sophisticated city and I knew my way around it, but New York was a totally new experience, and if I had thought about it I might have been frightened. But at the time I was in an anything-and-everything-goes frame of mind, and got right into the stream of the busy city. I felt I had made a sort of conquest; this first big city made me sure I could conquer others when the time came, and I did.

As I got off the train in Wilmington an M.P. came up to me, asked to see my pass and then gave me new orders. I was transferred right then to the Army Navy

General Hospital in Hot Springs, Arkansas. The hospital had a curriculum for laboratory technicians and I took all the course work offered. It was a well designed and practical course, with excellent instructors, so we had good training and could work in a hospital lab. The men who graduated with us went to hospital sections going overseas, as they could also be stretcher-bearers if necessary. All of the female lab-techs were kept stateside, yet all hospitals were still short of technicians. Letters from Hank eventually found me and several times Hank took the bus down, or hitch-hiked. Our relationship continued to deepen.

Shortly after my return to Wilmington our lab staff went to the beach for a picnic. I wasn't much of a swimmer but all of us enjoyed walking out to meet the surf of the cold Atlantic. It was low tide and the actual water line was a long way from where we had set up our tables. I stepped on something and then felt a sharp spreading pain on the top of my left foot, nearly knocking me to the ground. As I was a bit away from other people they didn't at first heed my calls, not realizing I was hurt. Finally, one of the guys came out to see what was going on. He called others and they carried me back to the eating area. Major Joe took one look at my foot, which was swelling rapidly, and handed me a fair sized paper cup filled with whisky, which he insisted I drink quickly. This was probably my first stiff drink, as I was still under age. One of the cars then took me back to the base, some ten miles distant. I vaguely remember going past the operating room where one of the surgeons came out and assessed my injury. He said a stingray had struck me and I was having a serious reaction to the injury. It was only a few days after a hurricane and stormy waters brought the stingray north. When I came to the next morning, I was in the bathtub and they were cutting my swimsuit off and getting rid of the sand. I was mighty sick and so out of it that I didn't really know what was going on.

Some of the lab crew knew I was seeing Hank frequently, so the doctors sent for him to come and informed my family as well. Hank got emergency leave and was able to stay several days. I seemed to be in a sort of fog but it was good to have Hank there with me. I had no idea it was such a serious injury but apparently the poison shot into me by the barb of the stingray made me very ill. The surgeon couldn't cut the barb out because of its location, just above my toes. It took some years for it to be totally absorbed. To my surprise it was a month before I was able to leave the hospital and return to duty. Hank came down each weekend I was in the hospital. We went to one of the dayrooms and listened to some classical music we both enjoyed. Otherwise we just visited and talked as I wasn't allowed to walk on the grounds.

On my twenty-first birthday, May 15th 1944, we went to Wrightsville Beach, where we bought sandwiches and pop at the store and then sat on a pile of logs on the shore. I was really shocked when Hank brought up the subject of marriage. He had bought a ring for me. Here was a man who wanted me. That was enough for me; since I had broken off with Harry my daydreams had never included the possibility of marriage. After surgery I had just assumed that I would never be asked to the altar. No one would want someone who couldn't give him a family. It was difficult to tell Hank that surgery had removed any possibility of my having children. I told him how great a loss this was for me, but I was emotionally unable to truly feel my loss, as it was still totally unprocessed; I was still stuffing things away, not being able to face them. In any case, we were not thinking of a family but just of ourselves and of the fact that war was soon going to part us. However, I remember talking even then about adoption and Hank readily agreed. So I made up my mind quickly that we had many common interests, and would no doubt make a good marriage. Hank made light of my not being able to have children; I doubt if he really processed it as he was just trying to encourage me to say yes to his proposal. Obviously each of us, caught in the moment, had little concern for the future.

Looking back, I guess I was like any other young person during those war years, with little common sense. Reflection also makes me realize that I had no idea what effect my surgery would have on marital relations. The thought had not ever crossed my mind so somehow I found a doctor, made an appointment, and haltingly asked questions. He really was little help; he had not ever had a patient with a similar problem. His only comment was to go ahead and see.

Hank and I were to be married on June 13, 1944 in Silver Springs, Maryland. Our furloughs did not jibe exactly so I arrived at his hometown of Clementon one day earlier than he. He had asked me to go to his parents' home when I arrived. I got off the bus in the small town, and found my way to their home, which was a large white two-story house on an acre of fully fenced land. I started to enter the gate but was stopped a large Chow dog whose barking, and bared teeth made me feel unwelcome. No one heard, I guess, so I walked back to town and stopped someone, asking how to get in. The gentleman kindly walked me back to the house and helped me get to the door safely. Hank's mother came to the door and said that Judy, for that was the dog's name, was harmless but there were no peace offerings on her part.

Hank's father was Austrian, his mother English and they met in England, married, and then came to the U.S. just after World War I. Hank's mother was small with wispy, long grey hair. She greeted me and showed me to my room. When Hank's dad came home later that evening we had dinner but somehow I wasn't very comfortable there. Hank looked a lot like his dad who was short, had a good head of grey hair and a ready, shy smile. The next day Hank arrived and together we talked with his parents about our upcoming marriage. Hank's parents seemed ancient as compared to mine, and hard to engage in conversation. They apparently lived quite a secluded lifestyle with his mother taking care of the house and garden and his father working in the restaurant business in nearby Philadelphia. On weekends they did the shopping and attended church in Silver Springs. I did not meet any of their friends and Hank remarked that they had always kept to themselves. At the time I did not realize the impact of such a narrow social life on Hank. This was such a marked contrast from my busy, outgoing family in California. I did not pay attention to the differences in our life style;

I was just caught up in the now, thinking that any fault or difference was easy to fix; anything was possible.

Silver Springs was Hank's home parish but because of my inability to have children we had to go to the Archdiocesan office in Camden to get papers signed. It was only then that I discovered Hank's real age made him eleven years older than I; he had given the impression he was in his early twenties. Dad couldn't get away from the ranch and Mother did not want to take the long train trip alone, so none of my family was present. My friend from Washington was to come, but last minute orders made it impossible. I had no one to support me or to talk with about my feelings. I think I probably didn't have enough courage to say "Wait". Only Hank's parents and a couple of Sisters who taught in the school were present when the priest married us after the daily Mass. We went back to the house for breakfast of very ordinary fare, no special wedding meal for us. Hank made an excuse, saying his mother wouldn't know what to prepare as she always cooked in the simple English way. Hank and I were both excited about our marriage but his parents' response was rather flat and unwelcoming.

Looking back on this special event I am aware that Hank's parents expressed no joy about our marriage. It was as if I was just taking their beloved son away from them. And of course this was true, as Hank paid markedly more attention to me than to them. Jealousy? No doubt they feared the future loss of Hank, not only because of marriage but the very real possibility of injury or death due to the war. I don't know what went on in their minds but it was evident I was so new an acquaintance that they didn't feel comfortable with me, nor I with them. I wasn't worried about this but only about our immediate lives together. A deeper relationship with his parents would just have to wait out the war. Hank and I were busy planning how we would get together on weekends. Sometimes I would go to Ft. Bragg and sometimes Hank would come down to Wilmington, or perhaps we could meet some place between.

We went on a week's honeymoon to Ocean City, N.J., returned to his home for a day and then went off to our respective bases. I have no idea whether or not our honeymoon was typical. We found a small hotel off the beach as we could not afford seaside ones. We actually had to show our marriage certificate to get the room, which shocked both of us. Neither of us had any real sexual experience so our ignorance got in the way of our first coming together. I was full of fear because of the experience with Jack, and then all the surgeries; I didn't know if I could feel anything. No doubt like many couples our lives had to grow together. We did find a sort of Bed and Breakfast in Wilmington and booked our space there week by week. Gradually, our intimate relationship grew to satisfy both of us; however, I am sure we were not the most innovative couple going.

Hank left for Europe very suddenly. We knew his division would go soon but the decision came more quickly than we had anticipated. He was not able to get a call through to me to say good-bye, but he got hold of one of my friends in Washington and she called to say he had left. I truly felt abandoned when I did not get a call or a telegram or any personal message. I had had only a couple of drinks in my life by then but I was hurting and angry at the war and without much thought I went to the Sergeant's Club with Barbara, a fellow lab tech, and had a mixture of rum and coke which really did me in. I had what must have been a hangover the next day. Both of us had to work. I drew the blood counts and pipetted them and Barbara counted them and somehow we sloughed off our other work and got through the day. I don't think I have ever been tempted to take that particular drink again.

In mid-December 1944, Mother was gravely ill, having had an ectopic pregnancy that was diagnosed only after emergency surgery. I knew mother had had her uterus removed a year or so before and shouldn't have been able to get pregnant, making the diagnosis difficult. She had given blood just the day before onset of this illness and after surgery she herself needed blood. Strange as it seems she received her own blood back as she had a rare type and hers was the only available match. A phone call from Dad helped me arrange an emergency leave to go to see her in the hospital, for her condition was touch and go.

If one flew on a commercial plane during the war it was quite likely a DC3 which was a twin-engine plane with seats for twenty-one. You had to have a priority to purchase a ticket. It took a full twenty-four hours to fly from Florida, stopping and changing planes in Texas, Denver, and Los Angeles. This was considered a fast trip. It was exciting arriving in the Denver airport in a snow storm. The landing was bumpy, scary, and as we slid along the runway, the plane nearly hit something near the runway. The pilots decided that if we were going to get out of Denver at all, we had to leave as soon as the plane gassed up. It was a tough decision for frightened passengers; some were so anxious about the weather they chose to wait in Denver. Only about six of us were willing to go on to Los Angeles. When we finally got there it was warm and sunny. Two scary flights so close together were enough for me. I took a southern route back East.

Mother was still in the hospital when I got there but gradually made a recovery. I stayed over Christmas to help with her care; she was very weak for quite a time so I took over preparation of Christmas dinner. When Hank was overseas we kept up a regular correspondence. As the war progressed I was able to figure out more or less where he was, including the Battle of the Bulge. I got no letters from Hank while I was in California and a call to a friend at the base verified there were no letters waiting for me. It was difficult to celebrate under the circumstances. Both Jack and Milo were in the Navy and Joy was away in school but joined us for Christmas.

Shortly after my return the Army sent me to Camp Blanding, Florida because there was a shortage of technicians there. Some of us used to roller skate to the wards as it was such a large hospital. I was on night duty for over a year starting at 4:30 in the afternoon and going to 7:00 the next morning. I did only emergency work so that gave me time for study. I had a bed for resting but if called, I had to scoot the cockroaches away before I could put my feet on the floor; we never found a way to get rid of them.

One adventure almost led to my arrest. Three-day passes were hard to get. Whenever we got a pass we tried to work it to an extra twenty-four hours by leaving the post a day early. I left one Thursday on an unexpected flight on a B 25 from Jacksonville, Florida to New York. I was really destined for Washington D.C. to visit my friend, but a short train ride would get me back from New York faster than I could get there by train from Jacksonville. There were seven of us and the pilot showed us the sites by flying low, about 500 to 600 feet, over Washington D.C. We could see the whole layout of the city; the spring flowers and plum blossoms were at their peak. We then headed for New York only to find out, en route, that we could not land there because of fog. The pilot was low on gas and decided to call another field for permission to land. When he went to use the radio he found out it wasn't working. He started flying very low looking for some place to land. The order came through to put on our parachutes. The pilot said if he couldn't find something soon he would turn us out to sea. We would have to abandon the plane out there, for he could not see the ground and was sure there were a great many houses in that area approaching New York. I was wearing a skirt so the Crew Chief took off his flying coverall and gave it to me to put on and then helped me into the parachute. I was really frightened but the men all knew their jobs and what they would have to do. Besides, being the only woman, and having often played rough with Jack, I just trusted that the men would tell me what to do and somehow I could do it. Finally, the pilot found an airport in the distance and without warning he landed. Immediately

132

MP's and other guards surrounded the plane. It seemed we had landed in Delaware on an unlisted site that was the staging area for planes taking off with air-borne troops for a parachute landing in France. We were hustled off the base quickly but still had one more river to cross. Our passes did not start until Friday so on the train to Washington I heard that MP's were coming through checking passes. I slipped into the Ladies and spent the rest of the trip there; no MP interrogation for me!

Once off the train, I was safe as they rarely checked passes when you were just walking about. I got to my friend's apartment, let myself in, and then decided to take a bath and sleep until she returned later that day. Next thing I knew there was a knock on the door. I had fallen asleep in the bathtub and the water was cold. End of my flights in army planes.

I guess wanting to be a doctor was still in me. One day the pathologist asked for a volunteer to assist at autopsies. I did this for a number of months. I was a good assistant and was interested in the whole process. The pathologist was willing to answer all my questions so we made a good team. Gruesome for sure, as I look back on it. For the life of me I can't figure out why I volunteered to do that work; I couldn't do it now.

The upper respiratory wards were furthest from the lab and we were called to get a blood count to verify a diagnosis of malaria. Most of the physicians on duty had never treated malaria but there were lots of cases of it as the men returned from foreign service. My training had included work with malaria slides but I still had to call a physician to verify slides. Doctors often mistook platelets for malaria so I had to convince them if their call was incorrect. It was important to get an accurate diagnosis so appropriate treatment could start.

During my service years I took many accredited correspondence courses from the University of California at Berkeley. These courses in economics, political science, history, psychology, and math were free to service personnel. I would study in the evenings as I waited for calls. I took thirty semester units, a full year. When I later applied for re-admission to Cal I received general units toward my degree because of all the specialized courses I had taken in the army.

I had a friend who owned a bookstore in San Francisco and he sent me the latest and best books on biochemistry, parasitology, bacteriology and other laboratory texts. So I did study in these texts under the supervision of the pathologist. Later I applied for and went to the 4th Service Command Laboratory Research Unit in Atlanta, Georgia for six weeks of training in parasitology. Many of the returning men from Asia and some from Europe had infestations of a variety of parasites and many also had unusual types of malaria, so this was important work for all of us.

As to the army life, well, I was quite a country hick as well as having led a somewhat sheltered life. I had little trouble with the women because I was more or less a loner, having only one or two good friends. I was still like two people, one with the steel container for my feelings and the unresolved issues with family, and another quite a competent, fun loving Sergeant who could and did work and play hard and would go the extra mile if needed. One could say that no one knew the real Jill, or her prior troubles; I never discussed them. The gambling or drinking crowds did not appeal to me at all. Of course, I had never lived in such quarters but seemed to get along and pulled as many shenanigans as the next one. I was already a good card player, became a good pool player, and used to cook Italian dishes with the pharmacy boys next to our lab. I had to stand less inspections, drill, and K. P. because of the work in the hospital. I slept at the hospital frequently but my space in the dorm was in a twin bedded room so I was quite comfortable.

Behind one of our laboratory buildings was a small pasture where our large ram lived. One of my chores, though we had several men in the lab, was to straddle the ram while the strongest men held him. I had to reach down and over and draw blood from his carotid artery to use for our needed lab tests. One day whoever was holding the ram let him loose too soon; he chased me but I ran for the fence and safety. One of the other girls was a total failure at this gymnastic procedure and the men wouldn't try at all. I guess there are some advantages to growing up a country hick.

Because of the war there were no regular weather reports. Often a hurricane would blow up without warning and be much worse than anticipated. I was in three major hurricanes, two in Florida and one in North Carolina. The WAC barracks where I lived was just across the street from the hospital. In the midst of a hurricane they wanted me at work; it was just too difficult to make the crossing alone so Sgt. Bostick came to get me. Bostick was about six-foot-two yet when we got outside, a strong gust nearly toppled us over.

135

He grabbed onto a telephone pole with one hand and held on to me with the other. We sort of squatted on the ground, in the pouring rain, for some minutes. Then, when it seemed calmer, we gingerly crossed on our hands and knees. I was drenched clear through but safe. I had to wear only my lab coat while my clothes dried. All of us stayed in the hospital for a couple of days as it was just too dangerous to make the crossing repeatedly. Of course we could eat in the hospital mess and made our coffee over the lab Bunsen burners. Even today when I watch the news my stomach lurches as I recall the feeling of helplessness of being out in such a storm.

The war was over during the time I was in Atlanta so I returned to Camp Blanding when my course was finished. Soon word began to surface about discharges. The basis was length of service, marital status, and the Army General Classification of our jobs. I had enough points for discharge because of being married and my length of service. My name appeared and I packed my bags to leave in mid-November but couldn't go, as there was a need for lab technicians. Then the word came that if your husband was returning from overseas service you could get an immediate discharge but that didn't work either. As Hank expected to return for discharge in early January I wanted to get out before he arrived. I called Dad and he spoke to Senator Knowland, who looked into the delay. It must have helped as I was discharged on January 1, 1946, from Fort Dix, New Jersey. I chose New Jersey as I could meet Hank there and I also got transportation money to get me back to California.

I went to Hank's parents' home and waited for Hank to come into Fort Dix the following week. I was quite uncomfortable, felt like an intruder being there on my own, so mostly just read during the day, waiting for the phone call to say where and when to meet him. When I talked with Hank's mother I found she had kept him tied to her apron strings; I wondered what would happen when he came back. He was certainly her son, not my husband.

I found out Hank would be arriving at Fort Dix very late at night so another friend drove me there. We went to a huge drill room where many others were waiting for their returning family members. I stood at one side and waited as soldier after soldier came through a single door looking all around for a familiar face. I wondered if this was really the spot where Hank was to come. Suddenly, there he was, coming through the doorway some fifty or more feet away. I spotted him straightaway but he didn't look the same, and of course he wasn't, after spending over a year in the rough of France and Germany. When he got closer I realized he looked older, terribly tired and I hoped it was just exhaustion that brought about the changes in his face and body. As we embraced I was aware of a stiffness on both our parts, but thought little about it because it was after midnight; our day had been extended and then some. He wanted to know where we were going to spend the night. Not knowing of his exact arrival I hadn't been able to make any plans but we stayed that night at one of the many guest dorms at the base. We went on the next day to Hank's home.

It was awkward visiting there because Hank's parents just assumed we would stay in the area permanently, but neither of us wanted to make a quick decision. Hank inquired and found out it was difficult to get into graduate school at either Villanova or the University of Pennsylvania as so many returning vets wanted more education. There would be no possibility of enrolment before fall and it was only very early January. We decided, perhaps at my suggestion, that before we settled down we should go to San Francisco to meet my family. We had some discharge money, plus savings from our meagre army salaries. It seemed as if all vets were on the move. We had money for either the plane or berths on the train but nothing was available. We traveled in uniform, with our "lame duck" discharge patches on our shoulders as neither of us had many civilian clothes. It took us five days to get from Philadelphia to San Francisco by train, sitting up and sleeping when we could. There my parents met us and we went on to the ranch. All I wanted was to get into a shower and into some clean clothes. Because I had so few clothes we went shopping only to find that not much was available due to clothing shortages. Hank had an easier time replenishing his wardrobe.

Mother and Dad were very hospitable but I knew we would only stay with them a short while. I felt a bit like a stranger in my home because of my marital status. I was glad my time in the Army was over, and just knew that I wanted to live in the West for a variety of reasons. One was that I still had viral pneumonia symptoms, with a cough exacerbated by coal smoke. So nothing drew me to the east, certainly not a winter in

Philadelphia or New Jersey; I was a westerner for sure. California's living expenses and lower university fees would make it less costly and we needed to be where we could manage on our own, without any family help or interference.

My relationship with the church and with God all these years showed little change. My prayer life during these Army years was very routine but consistent— morning and evening prayers, and Mass on Sunday. No special spiritual reading, as none was available. It never entered my head to think about a relationship with a loving God. I must say that sermons those days were of the vintage of, "thou shall not"; never inspiring.

Hank and I needed time and space to really get to know each other and living away from family would be good for us. Neither of us was very demonstrative and we kept searching for a comfortable life pattern. We decided to stay in California and go to the University of California at Berkeley. With his completed MA and his excellent academic record Hank entered the PhD program in English and started his courses while they sorted out his records and verified his acceptance. This was a lucky break as it took over six months to get the final acceptance but by then he was well into the second semester of work. The reasonable tuition in California made it possible to stretch the veteran's allowance to cover books. Both of us were eligible to receive government grants but it was a tight squeeze to make ends meet. After I finished a semester and a summer session I felt that Hank's education was more important than mine so I stopped classes, planning to return in the future.

All housing was terribly hard to find after the war and at first we lived in a three-room apartment in Richmond, about 350 square feet. Vets could rent it for $35.00 per month furnished, if you could call it that. Some years later, looking at old papers, I found we lived there for $125.00 per month for rent, phone, food, and transportation. Imagine. We kept looking for a better place to live because of the griminess and smell of nearby oil refineries. Finally, we found an apartment up in the Berkeley Hills. This was a lovely three-room apartment with a gorgeous view of the whole Bay Area, including Treasure Island and San Francisco.

When we arrived in California my friend Marilla told me that there was an upcoming State examination for laboratory technicians. I investigated and found that my college courses and years of work experience in the field made me eligible under a grandfather clause. I had less than two weeks to study but it was worth a try. Much to my surprise, I passed and thus became a Registered Laboratory Technician who could command a professional salary. My employment in a doctor's office helped Hank through his doctorate and gave us some extra money for cultural activities in the Bay Area as well as saving for a car.

One day my foot caught in a hole in the street not yet filled in after a re-paving. I fell, twisting my left knee, which required a cast for about six weeks. The apartment was up nearly a hundred steps; I could get up one step at a time, but going down required me to sit and bump down from step to step. Was I ever glad to get that cast off. Accidents had plagued me since early childhood. The after-effects of the many injuries began to have meaning now that I had reached adult-hood. Denial... as if I just could not be bothered to hurt. But it was different now that I had a husband; my responsibilities were no longer just to myself, I had to be more careful because anything happening to me impacted Hank.

Hank and I did have interests in common—music, art, history—and we always had plenty to talk about and share. Our life at UC Berkeley was one of preparation for Hank's career as an English professor. We visited a bit back and forth with a young couple, friends of mine who were also studying at Cal. Hank made a few friends in his classes, but mostly we kept a low-key social life because of studies.

Jean Bogert was a special older person in my life, a good friend from my teenage years whom I had met when she came as a guest to the ranch. Jean had a PhD in Biochemistry from Cornell and made her living writing texts in nutrition and chemistry for nurses. She lived at the Hotel Claremont in Berkeley. When Hank and I went to live in the Berkeley area Jean often invited us to the Claremont for Sunday brunch. We would also go with her to the musical events in Oakland or San Francisco as most often students received discounted tickets. We all enjoyed the return of the Swedish singer Kirsten Flagstaff, who gave her first concert after the war in Oakland. Operas and symphony concerts in San Francisco were other shared experiences.

Hank got his PhD at the end of summer, 1949. He sent his resume to Dominican College in San Rafael, California. They invited Hank for an interview, asking that I also accompany him. I bought a new hat to wear with my suit and white blouse. I carried gloves too. The President of the College and two other Sisters showed us around. I remember that we shifted walking partners so each of the Sisters was able to talk individually with us. I felt a bit strange being so interviewed but realize they wanted to be sure I would fit in with other faculty wives. When Hank came out of the President's office he said he had a job if he got his PhD before Dominican started in September. I was happy that Hank got finished in such a short time and we went over to Marin that fall to begin a real life.

September 2003. As I review this school era in my mind it is evident that even then we were growing apart. It takes a lot of concentration to get a PhD from a prestigious university in such a short time. Hank was content with his study, reading, and music. I often had lunch with friends who worked near the office so was more or less satisfied with my social life. Both of us were busy and tired and we never thought about or at least never discussed the need for more fun in our lives. Probably never gave much thought to how we neglected to work on our marriage. I guess I thought it would just happen. In some ways each of us was unable to share our real selves; emotionally closed but not aware of it. It is obvious that not doing the work of our marriage allowed us to get further apart as each of us got involved in our respective jobs. Building a home, but not growing at the same time. Not deliberately, it just happened.

Hank began teaching that fall as head of the Education Department at Dominican College. We rented a small, brand new house for $125 per month, with two bedrooms, and a fireplace in the living room. Two doctors hired me almost immediately as a laboratory technician for their office at a great salary. The Commencement and actual awarding of Hank's degree happened the next spring. The main speaker was President Harry Truman. My Grandma Ranker, a good Democrat, wanted to hear him speak so the two of us sat in the bleachers with some 99,000 spectators. We saw the line of the PhD's go forward to receive their degrees but could not pick Hank out. However, it was a great achievement and we were happy for him.

That spring Hank and I started looking for a house and bought our first home at 2 Southview Terrace in San Anselmo. G.I. loans were easily obtained and at a good rate of interest, so owning was cheaper than renting, just $105 per month including taxes. Our house had a large living/dining room, a kitchen, three bedrooms, and two baths upstairs. Ultimately, we finished the basement as a room and bath for Hal, our adopted son. The house had a large deck with a second fireplace and both this area and the living room had beautiful views of Mt. Tamalpais. We landscaped it that fall and then in February closed in the deck and put a cork floor down. We did all the work except for the roof, as we were far shorter of money than of energy.

Our Family Grows

As I mentioned earlier, I had told Hank that I was unable to have children; a real loss for me. At that time he said he would like to adopt children and as we settled into our home we applied to Catholic Social Service, stating that we would take older children if offered. There was the usual hassle about home inspection, a detailed history of our backgrounds, responsibilities, and finances. It was a fairly long process. In 1952 Eddie came into our lives; he was seven. The worker said he was a bright boy and needed placement quickly. The foster family where he had been living for three years had a boy about the same age who was in therapy and Eddie had to leave. Details were sketchy; and we found honesty and openness sorely lacking. It was just the day before he came that we knew he had been born with rosebud ears, an external ear malformation, but no hearing loss. Many complex surgeries, done by stages, totally reconstructed his outer ears and more surgery would no doubt be required. As if that wasn't enough, that same day we also heard that he was not yet available for adoption. A shock certainly, but as we had already planned his first visit we went ahead.

I was wondering what Eddie would be like and was eager for the doorbell to ring. Eddie shook hands and was at ease with us although we were total strangers. He had a wonderful smile and we immediately took to him. His eyes took in the whole room. No doubt his many questions and deep quest for knowledge reminded me of myself at his age.

We gave him a house tour and showed him his room. Eddie wanted to know where he would go to school so we took him on a drive downtown to see St. Anselm's school. He was full of questions about everything he saw; passing a bank he asked, "Is that where you keep your money?" I went on into the house with the social worker while the men stayed out to talk. Their discussion concerned pets; Eddie wanted a rabbit but Hank said he could only have a cat. I don't know if Hank even knew I was allergic to cats, but no matter, we were going to have one. The joy on Eddie's face made it imperative. He arrived to stay the day before Thanksgiving. He had a very small suitcase and a book in hand, one of the full-sized Oz books, which he was reading. I was amazed as he was only in Second Grade.

The next week we took him to the ranch to meet his grandparents. My Aunt Hilda was there and we had tried to fill him in on who he would likely meet. He walked right up to Hilda when introduced, put out his hand, bowed a bit and said, "Great-Aunt Hilda" and

145

some other greeting. We all burst into laughter for indeed Hilda had not expected such a title, though it was correct. He was so well mannered. My father took him to the barn where he chose Blackie. She was the mother of many kittens, including the one we kept until Eddie left home many years later. My allergies to cats continued, so Blackie was kept in Eddie's room or in the downstairs area.

One could say this was a new call from God. I knew that adoption was the only way I would have the privilege of being a mother. From the start Hank did not want infants; he was already forty, and quite sure an infant would not fit into our home as easily as older children. I knew that it would be special to really have children of our own and I was more than willing to assume the responsibility and life changes that would be required. An only child, Hank didn't have a clue about what changes would be necessary in our routines. The years of being a mother have been tremendously rewarding in spite of and often because of the fact that Eddie (now called Hal) and Jean are adopted.

So started our first weeks with Eddie! As far as I was concerned it didn't take me long to feel as if he had always been our son. I think I surprised myself with how good it felt to be a mother. This instant motherhood was in no way what I would have experienced with the birth of my own child but I knew that was impossible. I loved Eddie and later Jean as if I had birthed them. We needed to get a washer and dryer quickly as Eddie had a friend next door and, living in a newly developed area, there were many chances to get dirty. They found them all. Again a reminder of my own mud pie or creek experiences which brought me home with soaked and dirty clothes.

The first Christmas Eddie was shopping with me one day and saw a train set in the toy store. He asked, "Can a foster boy have such a gift?" Eddie of course knew he was a foster child and not yet adoptable. I said not likely, but that there would certainly be other good presents. We already had purchased a far bigger train set, mounted it on a board, slipped it under our bed, and brought it out at night when Hank worked with it; he cleverly built a whole village with a water tower, train station and other buildings one would find along a rail track. That Christmas Eve we went to midnight Mass and afterwards our friends Helen and Barney Mc-Grath stopped by for some goodies. The men moved the Christmas tree, put the train and its village down, then brought out the presents. But Hank had to show off his work and in so doing blew the train whistle. What a noise from the downstairs bedroom. We went down and there was Eddie jumping up and down on his bed, "I heard it, a train, a train!" He was upstairs like a shot and our night went well into morning. Both Hank and I were exceedingly happy at Eddie's reaction to his present, for the only thing he saw was the train; his other gifts still lay around unopened for hours. Eddie's delight in his unanticipated present, in fact in all of Christmas, seemed somehow to center him into our home and we were now a family.

When Eddie came we told him we wanted two children, the second a girl, if one was available. So the following May we heard about a seven year old girl, Sandra Jean who came one Saturday to visit. We de-

147

cided on a picnic, taking along a cake, as it was my birthday. As we gathered the food I asked her to open the olives. Her question, "Mother, how do you open the can?" startled me as I just assumed that she could do it. Suddenly, I realized she had called me Mother though it was the first time she had ever been at our house. She too wanted an immediate place in our family. On her next visit she wanted to change her name to Jean Marie, which she liked better than Sandra. She had been living in a foster home in Fairfax, quite close to us. We proposed that she visit us on weekends and move in with us when vacation came, but she wanted to come immediately. For six weeks or so I drove Jean back and forth to school. The first order of business was to get her hair cut and styled so we could see her beautiful face. In the fall she entered the Lower School at Dominican in Third Grade.

Two children nearly the same age, arriving so close together, demanded many changes in my life. I treasured the added sense of family and the challenge of helping them adjust to us, to each other, to new schools, and new relatives. Hank, as a child, was not involved in sports, music, or church activities. It became my job to do Cubs, Catholic Youth Organization and any activity related to school; the children attended different schools. I also continued to work at the orthopaedic office so my days were full indeed.

We adopted Jean in the minimum of one year and celebrated that day with a fancy doll cake. Although Eddie was not yet adoptable, we carefully made our wills so that each of the children would share equally if something happened to us. It was four or so years later

148

when I got a call at the office from a priest friend saying that the adoption could happen. I went to Eddie's school and told him; he got so excited I had to take him home with me. On arrival at home he announced that instead of Edward Thomas Aigner he was now going to be Henry Joseph Aigner, Jr., and from the time of the formal adoption he was Hal. Our friend Barney drew up the papers and Hal became our adopted son; all of us went to court for that event. We stopped at the bakery to get a cake that said, Happy Adoption Day, which the baker who also had adopted children gave Hal.

Hank and I eventually bought a house nearer Dominican. We all worked to put in the gardens, make a deck and a brick patio. This was a tremendous job as the kids and I hauled all the partial bricks from the kiln a few miles from home. The half-bricks were only a penny each so we could absorb the cost rather easily by doing all the work. A real family workout for all of us! When I drove by the house a few years ago our job still looked good and was level, which showed we had a good bed of sand as our base.

WOMAN

companionable   a listener
strength in times of stress

strong arms cradle
defend the young   helpless

touched by those in need
gives solace
supports quests
fumblings of growing persons

sparks others
kindles their life's thrusts

knows the emptiness of poverty
reflects God's light
carries her peace within
prayer

I always had two weeks vacation from work but much of the time Hank and I did not go away. We would take short trips to the beach, to San Francisco or other nearby spots, or up to the ranch. Like most young couples, money was always in short supply so if we went away we would often go with friends.

One Saturday during the summer I drove Hank and the children up to the ranch and left them there at the pink house. It was good to be back at the ranch but Hank was no outdoors man and none of the children there were the age of Hal and Jean. Hank didn't let them go off on their own as I might have done. I have always felt sorry that Hal and Jean did not get to explore the ranch and enjoy some of my special haunts but the time just wasn't there. I was often too tired on weekends to walk out into the hills.

Another weekend we were going to the ranch and hoping to stay a few days so we had to take Blackie and the new kittens with us. Hal got a good box, punched holes in it, and off we started. I was driving so am not aware of just what happened, but suddenly sharp claws were cutting into my legs, and I was going about fifty m.p.h, so I pulled over to the side of the road, yelled at Hal to hold the cat and off we went again. That night we fixed a box for Blackie and the kittens right next to Hal's bed. In the middle of the night he came into our room announcing that the kittens were missing. I cleared the sleep from my eyes, put my glasses on, yet still couldn't find them. There seemed to be no hiding place. Suddenly we heard a small sound from one of the dresser drawers, and there they were. How Blackie ever got them in there I don't know; but they stayed there and we all went back to bed. I am not happy with cats around, and certainly don't like to have my sleep disturbed by one; you can be sure that on the return trip Hal had everything under control.

In the summer of 1956 or '57, I experienced a terrifying incident when we took a drive down to Sausalito to see the old forts at the edge of the entrance to San Francisco Bay. We had gotten a new Chevy station wagon and were trying it out. I drove over some of the small roads on the point overlooking San Francisco, not really marked dirt roads, but with no Keep Out sign. Well, we should have kept out because suddenly I realized we were just a few feet from dropping several hundred feet to the ocean below. I was petrified. Needless to say I stopped quickly and felt terrible panic as we had not only our two children but also two nephews of Jean Bogert in the car. The car was so new to me I doubt if I had ever backed it up. I made everyone get out of the car and then took my heart in my hands and with a big prayer, slowly backed out of there. I was shaking. I don't think the children realized the extreme danger but Hank certainly did. My intuition, which has always been strong, saved us. This incident is one of many in which God intervened directly in my life, though I only realized it in hindsight.

✠

I was about thirty-three when I returned to college at Dominican, taking early morning or late afternoon classes while continuing to work full time. For practical reasons I majored in several subjects in college and was able to complete my fifth year for teaching. I did not start my career in teaching as there was no student-teaching supervisor at my level except for Hank, and that would never do.

It was a heavy load to work full time, take classes, and also have family responsibilities. Hank was helpful with chores and I did have the luxury of a cleaning lady once a week. I had been noticing some chest heaviness and pain when I was tired, or when walking up a hill following the kids. I had not seen a doctor for a real check-up in some years so went to an internist and was startled to learn that the chest pains were angina. I went on medication and immediately had to modify my working schedule.

I quit my full-time job and worked part time for Dr. Katherine Leicester, an Internist, doing laboratory work. I must say that the diagnosis of angina at age thirty-five really scared me though I did my best to hide it. At first I took so many nitro-glycerine pills that I was afraid I would explode, though they did relieve the chest discomfort. Treatment for high blood pressure put me on ever-changing medications. Overwork was certainly one of my problems but the most significant factor was the unacknowledged stress in our family.

Stress with Hank around our marriage and my attempt to hide these facts from myself had to play a big part in my illness. I was not yet able to look at what I put into or got out of our marriage; I knew it was flat but did not know why. I was afraid to look. I had a great deal to learn over the years. Hank began to be more anxious about all kinds of things; it was evident that two children brought major changes in our lives, including sacrifice of some of our personal time.

My friend Jean Bogert had never married so as the years passed and our friendship grew, we became her local family. Eventually, Jean bought a house in Belvedere to be nearer us and would spend special holidays with us. I helped her proofread some of her texts, especially the tables of food values for the appendix of her nutrition book. It was a painstaking job but we worked on it together and got it done. Jean asked me to take a trip with her to Vienna where she was to attend a conference. I helped make all the travel arrangements for the three-week vacation but Hank became seriously ill with his first bout of high blood pressure and I stayed home.

The next year Jean suggested that we all get on the ship in San Francisco, go through the Panama Canal to Europe, and then fly back. Again, Jean made all the arrangements for a two-month vacation for us but Hank's father became ill with cancer and died. His mother then came to live with us, making it impossible for us to go on the trip. I had been looking forward to a European tour and was frustrated that again we cancelled. I determined that someday I would experience the beauty of Europe.

The last year or two of Jean's life she had live-in help but I was responsible to see that she got all the care she needed. On the way home from school I often stopped for a visit. When she died I handled the arrangements and her brother and sister-in-law and niece came from Chicago. We had a very special, quiet service in her garden. Jean was a good friend and I missed this exceptional relationship. Our friendship had continued for nearly thirty years so Jean played a special role in my life. I was just seventeen when I first met her and she had been quite supportive of me when I was in college, in the service, and then during our years in Berkeley. She always encouraged me to get my education and then to use it for others. Our lives were totally different, yet the give and take of our conversations kept our friendship going. Over the years our relationship had changed. At first, I admired and looked up to her for all she had accomplished in her life. Then came a period where she was like a wise elder to me, actually part of our family, and then the last year or so when it was I whom she leaned on. Jean stipulated that some of the money she left to me was for a trip to Europe, as we had never been able to take a trip together. That trip was possible in 1976, but more about that later.

I have always been aware of some of my bad habits and, like most people, find them hard to break. When I first started working for Dr. Leicester in 1957 I often called myself stupid. She wanted to break me of this habit. Therefore, each time I referred to myself as stupid I had to put a dime in a special bank on my desk. As bright as I was, I still carried the message from my mother that I was not good enough, and a fine helped me break the habit.

That Christmas the Leicesters came by with some gifts. Among them was a beautiful tree of white desert holly covered with small red bows. On close scrutiny the bows each had a ten-cent piece attached. I thought this was a very clever way to give the children a bit of small change. Not so, Dr. Leicester said, "This is your present". I had forgotten about the bank at her office that had produced the dimes. I am sorry to say there were several dollars worth of dimes when I counted them, so you can probably guess I still had trouble getting rid of bad habits.

My worst habit, like that of many of my generation, was smoking. I had started smoking at about age fourteen and was smoking two packs a day by my early twenties. After the diagnosis of angina my doctor said I needed to stop smoking; I found it hard to quit. As a matter of fact it took some three months, starting and stopping, feeling like a failure whenever I allowed myself a smoke. The final result was worth it, for my pulse, which had been around 100 all the time, dropped to the low 70's.

155

February 28, 2001. Lord, help me to stop putting myself down; help me to be gentle with myself, help me to stop making strong judgments about myself, and voicing them, when I am not sure they are true. Mostly I do good things for others but need to be doing a bit more good for me.

I graduated from Dominican in May of 1958 and my only guests were Hal and Jean. Hank walked in procession with the faculty, so the children were by themselves. When we filed in I heard one of my children comment, "That's Mom." I heard someone in the audience chuckle. It was only then that I found out that I had graduated with honours. I was very happy to bring this formal degree work to an end and knew I would now be able to change careers some day. I wanted to have the same time off as Hank and the children enjoyed.

In the spring of 1960 Dominican added new faculty and I started my student-teaching at Edna Maguire, a middle school in Mill Valley. Just three weeks into student-teaching I had a job for the fall. Mostly I taught Math but also English and Science the first year. During all the time I was teaching I took classes from nearby universities, including several psychology courses that met all day Saturday for several weeks in a row. Some of these studies have been most helpful in my work in religious life.

November 2003. I liked teaching and I seemed to be good at it, to the surprise of many. Some friends thought my basic impatience would get in the way of effective work with children in a classroom. They were wrong. I found that the excitement of helping others to make discoveries on their own gave me all the patience I needed. Was my involvement with school a part of running away? Perhaps yes. Not running from specific household or family duties but hindsight tells me I was running from my inner turmoil and from unacknowledged awareness of dissatisfaction with my marriage.

Hank's parents never came out to California and neither Hank nor I ever visited New Jersey. About 1966 Hank's father developed cancer of the kidney and Hank went east just before his father died. He stayed on to empty the apartment and brought his mother to be with us since she could not live alone. We enlarged our house to give her privacy though she had all her meals with us. It was understandably difficult for her to cope with loss and the changes that came from being part of our busy life. I was out of the house from morning to evening five days a week but weekends were difficult, for we still wanted to lead a quite active social life.

My frustration and anger came out when Hank's mother ignored our rules about animals in the house. I was allergic to the cat, and did not wish the dog underfoot. Feeling ignored, I began to be loud and several times either one or the other of us had a short fuse. Hank often seemed to take his mother's side to make her happy, forgetting about his responsibility toward me. His mother expected Hank to make the rule changes she suggested. To me it felt as if I was a misfit in my own home, something I had previously felt when living in my childhood home. Hank and I had several discussions, some very heated, about the need for a greater level of peace in our home. Over the next year or so, it became too much for me, for all of us. After discussion with a priest friend, Hank agreed that his mother could get good care in another living situation and for our peace as a couple and family this had to happen.

We moved her into a Catholic care home in Oakland. She was there a year or so when, after an emergency hospitalization, we had her transferred to Marin General where she died of kidney disease. Now, years away from the situation, I can better relate to her feelings and the difficulties she had in making a transition to family living at her age. Coming from quiet surroundings to the hustle and bustle we enjoyed as a family was difficult for her. She loved animals and no doubt found comfort with them underfoot or in her lap. I could have done better if I hadn't been under too much pressure from other things. My fault.

✠

In the fall of 1966 I began to feel sick all the time. I didn't look sick, but I was tired, seemingly losing ground all the time and had great difficulty keeping up with my class preparation. I was a very involved teacher, approachable, and always ready to answer my students' many questions, but my lethargy made me irritable and I had to catch myself so I wouldn't answer questions too sharply. One day I went to the doctor, whom I had known for years, and just laid my head down on my hands on top of the desk and said, "Do something!" After more tests and difficulties I went into the hospital the day after Christmas for a liver biopsy. The next day the surgeon said I was indeed very ill with a much enlarged liver, which had a seriously high fat level. They investigated the possibility of poisons and chemicals I might have come in contact with but were never able to find the actual cause. Bed rest was the immediate treatment and I stopped teaching for the next six months, which were followed by summer vacation. It was a tough time as Hank had high blood pressure and pills weren't what they are today. He had been in the hospital the previous summer for over two weeks before they got his blood pressure under control.

As I came into the house from the hospital Hank spoke of how fearful he was about my not being able to work, afraid that we couldn't make it without my salary. We didn't have back bills so this really hurt, as I knew the serious nature of this illness and also knew that its outcome was uncertain. I felt as though the work I could do, the money I could make was what mattered, but I did not matter. Again God was watching over me but I did not feel God's loving care, which I desperately needed at the time. I didn't know how to beg God and it's so hard to pray when one is so ill.

August 2005. It has taken years to sort out this illness and its consequences. When I came home that December day I was in shock, nearly a basket case. The doctors told me there was no way to know if I would ever get over the liver problem. Time alone would answer that question. Hank's fear was so great, he was not able to empathize with my turmoil. What I needed right then were strong arms to hold me tight, to put me together again. Hank was not able to fulfill that role for me. No doubt, if I am brutally honest, I was so darn independent most of the time that I gave him mixed messages and he did not know my need nor understand my hidden anxiety. Once again my own past got in the way of creating more appropriate life patterns.

My illness put me to bed and placed a burden on Hank and the children. I wasn't able to do anything for at least three months, so Hank shopped and he and the children got the meals. Quiet and rest were essential for my recovery. I tried as much as possible to have my mornings without any interruption, asking Hank and the children to get their needs met when I was in the family room. Hank had real difficulty following this suggestion and day after day would find excuses to come into the room to look for something or ask me an unnecessary question. I got very angry one day and said his trumped up excuses would have to go and if need be I would put a strong lock on the inside of the door. On reflection, I realize he was just anxious and needed the assurance I was still there and really all right. But I was ill and my basic need was to be alone in the morning.

This time was one of the lowest points of my life. I had realized for some time that I was disillusioned with my husband; the protector I saw in Hank at our first meeting was gone. This man was frightened and distant. His anxiety over my illness and the future came across each time I saw him. He had lost the zip he had before his stint in Europe during the war. I was frightened about my own future and Hank's lack of response to me just made me become more independent.

The years of doing had just reinforced my strong independent bent and it was evident, if I was honest, that I could carry on without Hank's help. Maybe the eleven years difference in our age was beginning to show. My days had been so full that there was no time or quiet for just taking an honest look at where and how we were together as a couple. Neither of us expressed our fears to the other but muddled along as best we could. I kept my disenchantment with Hank locked in, keeping all my worst fears deeply inside. I was falling out of love, or at least recognizing a significant change in our relationship, and becoming aware of the fact that we didn't have a meaningful one.

As time passed I began to feel a bit better physically and began to sort out what was really going on in my marriage. Each of us, in our own way, contributed to its failure. For my part I again felt abandoned, angry, and frustrated. Hank seemingly had no understanding of the seriousness of my illness. I learned I couldn't depend on him for real support or help; his work, being a parent, and his fears used up all his energy. We were not at all able to communicate honestly and openly about our individual physical and emotional problems.

I knew that we needed a professional counsellor but Hank refused, not being able to accept that there was a problem. Denial all around! In a sense this time away from work, with time for reflection, allowed me to grow up and look not only at my marriage but at my whole life. Was I really living and working at building up our family unit? Was I blaming the situation on Hank; was I taking my share of responsibility? These questions were deep within, but difficult for me to share. I guess I wasn't ready for the drastic changes that would have to occur before I could hear what I needed to do. I also needed a good dose of courage.

HEALING

To be healed means
To become God's image of me

life can blow past
me unless I encounter it
surrender to God's life within.

I search, seek, hunger, long for peace
lonely, there is a longing without form
aimless reaching out   searching
know not my direction

In sorrow, depression
turn in on myself
God understands anxiousness
forgives   brings a healing touch

Letting go of all
turning over all to God
already being healed

God knows the hardness of my heart
my tears of sorrow
God melts my heart.
Deep within
in the unique cells of my being

Does life burst forth   surge into me
or am I a barrier
to the healing power of life?

The healed person is beautiful
colored by experiences of sorrow   healing
of life lived seeking peace.

Healed, I accept whatever comes
Presence within

TRIALS AND TROUBLES

By fall my liver function tests approached normal, my energy had gradually returned and I was ready to teach again. I asked for Fifth Grade in one of the grammar schools. I found it a whole new experience, working with just one group of children, and hoped to spend my future there. I enjoyed that age group and my creativity and skills were tested. In my second year my class constructed a doll house following the plans from *Sunset* magazine. This was a spare-time activity, one which helped students finish their work quickly. The students did math, carpentry, and painting and made ingenuous furnishings as they learned new skills. This was a most successful doll house which delighted the First Graders who were its recipients.

After two years I returned to Edna Maguire to take on the responsibility for the math program for the whole school. Teaching at that level involved students with a wide range of abilities; some were in Fourth Grade math, others at their actual grade level, with the top students finishing algebra and geometry.

When I drove to school in Mill Valley I took the back road, and stopped at St. Patrick's church in Larkspur for Mass, which was a great settling influence for me. It is obvious that I was searching for something I did not have, a depth of relationship with God, a sense of peace, at least at the start of the day. However, my participation was such that it was a head trip, not one which touched my heart. What was I expecting? In truth I did not know, I just felt there was more to church than I was getting and I sensed a need not yet met. Of course, if I didn't go then there would never be an answer to my questions.

One day I was called to the office to take a phone call from Dad. He said he needed me because Jack had died suddenly of a blood clot. Jack had been in a terrible accident on the ranch about ten days earlier, when a jeep he was driving up the mountain turned over and crushed his pelvis. I had not gone to see him because Dad had said he was making a good recovery until the clotting ended his life.

> November 2003. Jack and I hadn't talked about the sexual abuse for perhaps twenty-five or more years but it was still a blot in my life, a big black one. Looking back I realize two very significant events took place. One is that Dad called me rather than others to help him make decisions. Secondly, within the next three days the whole memory of Jack's abuse and its effect upon me

nearly broke me at his grave. I remember sitting at the gravesite as the gun salute sounded and taps played and bitterly saying to myself that I was glad he was out of my life. I thought I would be free as a result of his death, but I was not. It took more counselling, growth work, prayer, and time to really forgive Jack. I haven't forgotten what occurred so long ago though it is now healed and in proper perspective among other life events.

RECONCILIATION

Death
invisible   insights
in darkness come.

Led in trust
faith
beyondness

Reconciliation
speaks forth
generates new life

The next several years brought more changes to our family, some easy and some hard to bear. Hal graduated from San Rafael High and went on to Marin Junior College, driving the short distance. Jean had been dating a classmate for a couple of years. Both Hank and I were very upset, as we knew Ron had serious problems with alcohol. We hoped we could help Jean see that the relationship with Ron needed to change. After long discussion we all decided Jean could board at my old school, the Ursuline Convent in Santa Rosa. She continued to see Ron on the sly, so in Twelfth Grade she drove to school daily. Immediately after graduation Jean got a job with the local telephone company and moved to an apartment in downtown San Rafael.

When Ron and Jean decided to get married they went to the local priest to set a date. The priest called us in to sign the permission required for minors to marry. We had a very long and difficult talk with the priest and I refused to sign. I did not approve and the priest's attempts to make me change my mind were to no avail. Hank wasn't as vehement but also decided not to sign. Jean married Ron in a non-Catholic ceremony but neither of us attended the wedding. They had two sons, Rodney and Anthony. Ron continued to have problems and when the children were both small, he and Jean divorced.

I felt totally inadequate as a mother; it was not possible to get Jean to see Ron's serious problem. Only rarely did I see Jean after her marriage but I did hold my first grandson, Rodney, when he was just five days old and later Andy, when he came along. Our visits were sparse and I tried to support Jean as best I could, but feel I did not have the skills to really be of help. My own unhealed woundedness got in the way.

Shortly after Jean's divorce she met Vern Leete of Santa Rosa, a single parent with two girls and two boys. They married and raised her two, his four, and two more girls that they had together. This family blended well and now all are adults with children of their own. I miss seeing my grandchildren and great-grandchildren and perhaps someday I will spend time with them. Jean and Vern are good grandparents and now are looking forward to their own retirement.

Jean and Vern became Mormons many years ago and they and their children are all very active in that church. It has been hard for the children to have a grandmother who is both Catholic and a Benedictine Sister. Jean has visited me here in Nanaimo a few times, and came to my Twenty-fifth Jubilee. I am sorry that they all live in Utah, Atlanta or spots on the East Coast and my visits with them are few, though I do see Jean at family meetings. She and I talk fairly frequently and the pain of so many years ago is gone. Currently Jean is training to do a mission in the Mormon Church. This, according to Jean, came about in part because of my example of volunteer work and then my commitment as a Benedictine Sister. This warmed my heart and I am sure God is blessing her work and mine too.

After Hal finished University, he was a free-lance writer for many years, as well as a carpenter for his friends on the boardwalk. He went on to law school and became a lawyer. He found practicing law often brought him into conflict with some of his ethical standards. He has now found his special place as head of the Law Library in Marin County. He is a wonderful, generous, caring man and I am proud to be his mom. He has never married.

The start of some eighteen years of retreats that I made at the Cenacle Retreat House near Sacramento came about at the invitation of a friend. The Cenacle Sisters, an international order, were founded to work in the retreat ministry. When I first went there I made many silent retreats, directed by Cenacle Sisters. They have always worked closely with Jesuits in offering a wide variety of retreats. The most memorable were two retreats with Father John Powell, S.J., who was working on his book, *Why Am I Afraid to Love*. Father Powell talked, four times a day, for eight days about love. He was a great retreat master and also a good spiritual counsellor. I started to read widely about spirituality, especially books by Thomas Merton and Teilhard de Chardin. There were also many opportunities to attend lectures at Dominican and at the University of San Francisco.

With continued study and reading all those years my head got full of information even if my heart didn't absorb it. By this I mean I did not feel the love of God in my heart. I felt I was unlovable, certainly a carry-over from my childhood. I had opportunities for spiritual counsel from the Sisters, but couldn't take it in deeply enough to become free, allowing God's love to soak in. Facts such as God loves you, came into my mind and sat there. I had no tools to use in taking these facts to my heart. I just had not developed the relationship with God which made this possible and honestly did not know that there was a whole other way of relating to God.

A special retreat for me was one with Father Anthony DeMello, S.J., who was from India and anyone experiencing his retreats and groups came away more aware of the beauty and sacredness of life, all life, everywhere. Hank and I had an unusual opportunity to be with him when we showed him San Francisco. He came down by bus and we met him at the bus depot, took him around the city, and then drove over the Golden Gate Bridge to have lunch on the waterfront in Sausalito. He asked me if we could go up into the fog. Well, San Francisco had plenty of it that summer day, just up at the top of one of the hills. I stopped the car and Father De Mello stepped out, opened his hands, and allowed himself to experience not only the sudden change in temperature but also the dampness. He said he had wanted to feel the fog, a new experience for him, and I must say I had felt it many ways before but never with the obvious delight I saw on his face. It was a shock to all of us who had experienced this unusually gifted man to hear of his sudden death from a heart attack when he was only in his early fifties. This was long ago but De Mello's work lives on, through the many reprints of his books, as well as through groups that follow his suggestions for meditation.

Gradually over the years the emptiness, the longing for something I did not have, kept drawing me to make retreats in the hope of a deeper relationship with God. Sometimes when I just couldn't stand the stress at home, the upsets with Jean or the growing distance between Hank and me, I would take a long weekend and drive up to the Cenacle. I might or might not attend the weekend retreat, except for Mass, but I would walk around the beautiful grounds, perhaps talk with one of the Sisters, read and try to pray.

August 2003. Many times during retreats I tried to grasp a deeper understanding and acceptance of God's unconditional love. This pointed out some strong truths for me. I was already a very aging adult and had lived over half my life, before the truth of God's love and forgiveness for me wiped away any list of judgment on His/Her part. Why did it take so long? Well, as I now know, I got God all wrong and because I did not recognize the problem, I did not own it, work with it, or replace it with another image. I knew nothing of a loving God within my deeper self.

This gradual freeing of God to act in my life, my own removal of the unknown barriers I had put up, presented me with many unanswered questions. I did not feel worthy of love, God's or that of anyone else. I most probably need to say I did not have an inkling about what love was. I am aware that Father Powell's retreat on LOVE just didn't really open the ears of my heart.

Looking back I would say that the spiritual directors I saw at the retreat house just didn't get my dilemma. I again didn't know what I didn't know. I could read the words, understand in my head, but it is now obvious to me that the Presence of God in my life and any sort of meaningful relationship just did not take place. I know my reticence and my inner turmoil put up a barrier to a deeper understanding. Not yet ready, I needed to work in other areas, and face myself and what was going on in all realms of my life. Perhaps I was just good at hiding the real issues, even from myself. I also was not able to trust another person enough to present questions which, when answered, might well have solved my God/ me prayer impasse. I didn't have the language to ask the questions without feeling like a fool; at my age, my very basic questions seemed ridiculous.

No one talking to me would think of my need for the most basic instructions in prayer and God relationships. They assumed I learned at my mother's knee, just as they did, in their Catholic homes. The God of my early childhood was not my friend or companion. I had good head knowledge from my reading and retreats but lacked the fundamental understanding that God loves me and that God is present in every minute of my life. I talked a good line but didn't feel presence at all. So, I lacked support which I so desperately needed.

I did not know how to put my questions to any of the Sisters. I was ashamed of the poverty of my ability to love God or let God love me. Pride? Stubbornness? Do it myself? All were areas which clouded my personal growth. I did not have any one director consistently, so the barrier was not broken until late in life.

As I myself worked in spiritual direction, my own fumblings and areas of growth helped me to be more compassionate with others and I could also help them to voice their own questions.

I have a pattern, a life-long one, of needing to be away by myself when troubled. I need time to sort things out in a safe place. The contours and other spots were safe nests for me when I was at the ranch; the Cenacle became a safe place for me for over eighteen years. Now I have another hide-out, a run-to spot where I can be all by myself.

SILENCE

Silence in words   prayer
in the darkness of the mind's eye
speaks of loneliness aloneness   presence.

True silence, stillness
unaware of myself .
the walls of my heart
echo the sound of presence.

God created me to be silent
to listen   to hear
serenity comes to the core of my being.

Cloaked in true silence
I am nourished by God's word
presence.

Stillness, like darkness
magnifies the most minute sound
God's creative touch.

I see a drop of water
hear its sound
I am expanded
called beyond myself.

In the summer of 1969, I drove up to the Vancouver,
B.C. Cenacle to make a retreat and try to discern the
direction of my marriage. Hal had gone on to further
education and Jean had married. I told Hank of my
need to stay away most of the summer and tried to express my honest feelings about our marriage but I doubt
if it got across. I stayed for six weeks in a motel getting
my own meals, spending hours walking, reading, and
trying to sort out my life. I wanted to be on my own,
to experience what that would be like for me.

I took some short trips from Vancouver and also flew
from Vancouver by plane to Whitehorse in the Yukon.
I knew that Jack London had been in Whitehorse and
thought it would be interesting to visit there and go
across to Skagway by train. That evening I took a trip
up the Yukon River where there was a sign across the
river at one point which said: *Jack London was a bar
pilot on this river in 1898.* It was perhaps ten o'clock
at night but as I was so far north it was possible to
read nearly twenty-four hours a day. The sights I saw in
July were quite different from those experienced by the
men who prospected for gold or piloted on the river.
Their hardships, overcrowded living conditions, lack of

food, lawlessness and "gold fever" are all gone; White-horse has most of the amenities of a small modern city with shops, roads, hotels and policing as well. Some of Jack London's novels, *Call of the Wild*, *White Fang*, and numerous short stories and articles had their start in the winters of this rather uninhabited land. From the Yukon I went on the train across to Skagway, noting the trees dwarfed by the elevation and the chill of the far north. I joined a small cruise ship in Skagway and travelled to the ice fields, saw First Nations dancers at Haines, then on to Juneau, Alert Bay and other stops along the British Columbia coast to Vancouver. Great fun. I returned to Vancouver and spent a week or so there, then drove home. The only decision I made was to seek more professional counselling, hoping that now Hank would join me.

It's hard for me to write about my relationship with Hank. As I said earlier in my story, we met and were married during the war. Many young service people lived on the edge, living as if there would be no second chance. I don't fully subscribe to that, in fact Hank and I corresponded quite a bit, talked several times on the phone and had occasional visits before we got engaged. We were not any more foolhardy than others in war-time, but got caught in wanting to share a bit of life be-fore he left for overseas. We felt we had many interests in common, were free to marry and so we did.

Hindsight and reflection on the timing of my mar-riage shows me that I was no doubt on the rebound from two things; the break up with Harry, and the extensive surgery. I did not really allow my intuitive sense to operate, just went headlong into marriage. I was running!

When we lived in Berkeley we were students with deadlines, long hours of study for Hank, and work and the house for me. When we moved to Marin we were both busy working and getting a start on our home. Then the children came, adding to our joy and also to our involvement outside the home. There are just tons of things one has to do with children and Hank did not fully engage in this part of parenting. At one time both kids were in some form of Scouts, Hal a Cub Scout and Jean in Campfire. We had friends who had children near their ages so we had some joint activities with them; I was busy working full time, caring for a house and taking the children to activities. Two lively seven-year-olds joining our family within a few months brought real change in our own personal lives, obviously more for Hank than for me. The stresses with work, school, my heart condition followed by a serious liver ailment and a couple more surgeries, were not helpful. Hank too had illness and the prescribed medicines were ineffective. Hindsight tells me we gradually grew apart, even our relationship to God and involvement in our religion was quite different. Hank was a born Catholic and certainly was a well informed one. He was reticent to talk about his faith, but read about it as well as attending Mass weekly.

I became interested in personal growth and went much more frequently to retreats, psychological lectures, and spiritual growth workshops as well as taking classes that would help with issues that came up for me. Hank was just not interested in the changes

177

brought forth after Vatican II. Perhaps he felt he had enough input by sharing with other faculty members. He wouldn't go with me to lectures by Carl Rogers, Rollo May, Fritz Perls and others who came to the Bay Area.

It was only after a long time that Hank agreed to go for couples' counselling. The counsellor suggested Hank go for some individual work but he went a time or two and would not continue. At no time was he open to discussing his feelings, often seemed not to be aware of them. He kept saying our marriage was just fine and I have to accept that he spoke his truth. However, it wasn't working at all for me and I felt no support at a very pivotal point in my life. We had just grown too far apart for me to see how we could continue with our partnership. Hank just seemed old and not interested in the now and the future. Perhaps too many problems faced him and he was not willing to get help.

As we sat on logs at Wrightsville beach early in our relationship, we talked about things with real meaning. We bared our souls, as it were, mostly about what we liked about our lives. We shared much about music and art and books and thought about a future together. We certainly shared about what we might expect to enjoy when the war was over. The war changed both of us. There was a growing barrier between us and we never regained the flow and depth of sharing we had before Hank's overseas experiences.

Though we were not aware of it at the time, apparently something happened to each of us. To me, Hank seemed far quieter, more cautious, and wanting to be by himself, reading or listening to music. This had been

178

his pattern, he said, all through school and his teaching experience. He was a loner, not really needing to be close to anyone. It was hard to draw him into conversation, particularly about feelings; I was little better. I think neither of us woke up to the fact that we were not working on our marriage. Unfortunately, we were not able to touch each other in depth. Our lives became like railroad tracks, each going on a parallel journey with a sudden split in the rails and in our life as a couple.

Hank and I attended a couples' retreat given by a Marist priest who was studying under Virginia Satir in San Francisco. We talked with him and found he was living at the Marist house only a few blocks from our home. He agreed to take us as clients if we would both see him, either individually or as a couple, as indicated by our progress. We continued to see him on a regular basis for about eight months. He helped us look at our relationship, call it dysfunctional, and helped us see that we had grown to a point where our marriage would probably break up. In fact, it was already dead.

Working with a priest as a counsellor helped me to let go of the stigma of leaving Hank. At that time few Catholics were separating or divorcing, tending just to make do as best they could. We had been married for over twenty-five years but the tension of the marriage was just too great for me to handle; a break seemed inevitable, if I was to survive. For several weeks I knew this truth, but could not act on it.

One day the counsellor asked us to take trust walks. I blindfolded Hank and we took off, he holding my hand and following my instructions. We arrived back safely having traversed the ground floor of the entire building. It was my turn next. Immediately, Hank telegraphed his lack of assurance in leading me. It was as if he could not depend on his own ability to take charge. I tried for a bit but his unease made me stop. I found I could not go on with the exercise. The counsellor really challenged me for not following Hank and letting him do his job. I said I just couldn't. I realized I did not trust him at all in such situations, feeling terribly out of control and shaky as a result of the experience. We talked at length about this episode.

Time has made me aware of the poverty of our communication skills. Trust was obviously a strong problem for me. It was also apparent that I judged Hank and of course, this wasn't the first time I had done that. We had had many months of counselling when, just at the end of the session one day, the priest asked me what I was going to do. I said, "Leave". Hank pleaded with me to stay, saying he would do anything just to have me stay, but I knew it wouldn't work.

November 2002. Hank and I separated more than a quarter-century ago, which has given me time to evaluate that step, or misstep in my life. I am not sorry I married but am sorry I was not able to fulfill the commitment I made. I had stopped growing in our relationship. I am not proud of that, but my leave-taking only reiterated the basic need for survival. I chose life as a single person. However, my married years gave me a better understanding of life as others face it, which has been very helpful in my work as a spiritual director.

Hank was an only child with older parents who were living an isolated life in a small town near Philadelphia. They were Catholic and all his education was in Catholic schools, as was his teaching experience. I came from a quasi-Protestant family with a large extended family making a daily impact on my life. Socially, I was way more adept and needed to continue with an active social life, which I am sure was quite hard on Hank. At times Hank felt burdened because of the needs of the children. He had to make many more adjustments to life with children than I, though I was slow to become aware of all our differences in outlook on life.

I could add that when one works as hard as I did, teaching and taking classes and running a home and social life, there is just no time for personal growth; I was unaware that I needed to schedule growth time into my routine. The same is true if couples are to continue in a good relationship. I was remiss in not putting higher priorities on marriage issues; but no one challenged me to do so until it was too late. Death had already crept in, unbeknownst to me. I couldn't rekindle the flame and perhaps in all honesty it seemed impossible because Hank saw no need for our life to change.

TO LIVE IS TO DIE

To live is to die
to die is to change

Be fully alive means partially dead
dead to self
to live is to struggle
die more completely

I leap up   gain God's love
give it totally away
giving all I have received
more full than ever

Coldness, void, death
yet the call so clear
warms me
makes me eager to respond

Death, total fullness
beyond my capacity to understand

I am afraid to let go
go with God to be born anew
As I give of my true self   very nature
dying takes place

In giving... dying
life's strands
bent   broken
out of containment.

A dying breath
life replaced by death
that very instant God takes over
resurrection   new life

Was I just hearing a call to be me? Was I waking up to a change of my way of life? Not only the where or how of earning my living, but all my future could, and probably would, change; a call to be me more as God made me, if I would take the responsibility to listen, to make it happen. Time to be true to myself led me to search deeply at a leisurely, uninterrupted pace. It was like I sat in my body, in my chair, and deliberately opened myself to allow change to come from any direction. This gave me a unique opportunity to put on a new skin, to redirect my life. From the first day I felt I had abandoned some of my former self. I was unhooked from my former ways. Scary, yes, as I was aware of not knowing myself deeply enough. Immediately, my pace of life changed. I was in charge; I didn't even ask the questions as to when and where and why. Release from tension. I relished the quiet, the freedom to come and go, fix meals or go to bed; simple decisions, but different, outside the marriage setting. Reflective quiet began to heal the pain from leave-taking.

It took nearly three years before I settled into a new way of life, one that I had never thought of before. I was not sure that it was the right kind of life for me, but it was a call and I heard it loud and clear. Interesting, that as I write this and say "loud and clear" I remember that the actual voice was quiet, wistful, and gently asking me to try a new way. I did, and the voice has continued to be quiet, persistent, and beckons me to follow. I received the support to live each day as it came. Often unsure and bewildered, but willing to go on.

My first forty-six years were lived in the pattern to which I was born; university, a good profession, marriage and children. A good suburban wife and mother. It has been thirty-five years since I walked out of my home, and I know deep within that I not only heard a voice then, but that it has been one continuous call through thick and thin. I have changed, now there is time for knowing myself and God's unconditional love for me, for sharing the fruit of that relationship with others.

In a sense, the next three years were between lives... This was a time like the gradual darkness that descends as twilight comes, yet I had a deep assurance that a dawning wasn't far behind. A good-bye... followed by a hello. A beginning of a beginning! Somehow, I just knew that God would reveal the direction. These years were not easy, a radical change from my former life but I was growing toward wholeness and peace.

ALONE

I packed a few clothes that evening and left for good the next morning, not certain where I was going. I knew I needed an apartment fairly close to my work. I had made no plans about how I would get from one day to the next. I was in a fog. I called a friend in Berkeley and stayed in their guest room above the garage. For two days I just slept and tried to recoup from the shattering experiences of the last few days. I returned to pick up more personal items and clothing when I knew Hank was teaching a class. Home was a motel until I found an apartment.

I had never anticipated what would be required if I left. I had been too busy just trying to make the decision to leave. The shock finally hit a couple of days later as I allowed myself to look at the extent of all that faced me. Changes of address, bank accounts, auto insurance, subscriptions, as well as informing family and friends—these were the immediate problems I had to solve. I had chosen to just leave, letting Hank have all the furniture, in fact, all of our things, saying that I could come back later and decide what I wanted and needed to take with me. I had to furnish an apartment from start to finish. Gradually, I got things sorted out but my most immediate need was to get myself together enough so I could go on teaching. I took only two days off plus a weekend, a foolish decision, but I wanted to appear strong and in control so friends wouldn't ask too many questions I didn't want to answer.

January 2004. Reflection says that here, once again, is a pattern from earliest childhood. It's as if once I had decided to leave, taken the step, I just stood there and took a beating without crying. The difference was that now I had the strength and the independence and was able to pull my life together. I didn't know what I would change, but I knew that the future was not my mother's, nor Hank's nor anyone's, just mine. I willingly took responsibility into my own hands, something I was not fully able to do before this time.

I still wasn't sure that I was being fair, just, or correct but I knew I was dying and all the help that I received pointed out my direction—leave and take on a future not yet known. It took years to realize that one always suffers from mistakes, but ultimately one handles them so that life can go on. I did my best. No longer a victim but a survivor. In furnishing my new apartment I had need of household linens so I went to a large department store to buy them. I picked out some kitchen towels and dish cloths and took them to the counter and asked that they charge them. Immediately I had to go to the Credit Office about my account. "Your account has been closed", I was told. It was their policy to close all accounts of those who were divorced. Angry, I explained that the account had always been mine, not my husband's, and that I had steady employment at a high salary in the Mill Valley School District. No matter, they closed it. I was appalled at the policy being automatic and so high-handed, so unjust. I never bought another thing in that store. This was the first of many awakenings to the business world's treatment of divorced or separated people, especially women.

We had made satisfactory arrangements about finances and our material goods. We decided to just get a legal separation, as neither of us intended to remarry and Hank did not want the stigma of a divorce. I did not apply for any kind of church annulment. Hank's reaction to my leaving was disbelief. He apparently had never been able to hear what I was saying, even right to the day I left. As soon as I got my apartment in Greenbrae he would drop by with a piece of mail or a bill that needed attention from me, or some other excuse to ring the bell. For weeks he pleaded with me to reconsider. I finally established some strong boundaries, asking him to just forward all mail and if necessary, to contact me by letter. I got an unlisted phone, which also helped.

March 2004. Because we kept silent about the underlying causes of the breakdown of our relationship it came as a shock to most people. We shared only with professionals who could give us help as we struggled through our relationship and the decisions we had to make. I kept on far too long for my own good, but shame, weakness, and ineptness kept me in the marriage. It was only when I started to deeply consider the facts as I myself presented them to the counsellor and he played them back to me, that I could at last make the decision to leave. It was hardest to tell the children, and Jean especially, was stunned and upset. Hal, who had lived at home longer than Jean said, "I know how hard it has been for you." Hank needed to stay in the area because of his job but I was able to move away and still continue with my work in Mill Valley. Today I know that the decision reached so many years ago was a good one. I am sure now that God gave me a bundle of strength which sustained me in my decision.

After Hank and I separated the two of us never talked about these most difficult choices. As far as I was concerned, the decision in the counsellor's office was final. Each of us had to find our own level of peace. When I visited Hank in his apartment in Santa Rosa years later, close to the time of his death, he told me he still had strong feelings about our relationship. It was not hard to visit Hank; he seemed older, but was gracious and friendly, yet it was obvious that we had changed since our last encounter when each of us still felt the shock of our separation. My feelings toward him were those of compassion and sorrow.

Hank continued on at Dominican, working until he was seventy-two. He lived on into his eighties. Over the years our children and my parents continued to see Hank but I saw him only at the funerals of my parents or family members and, as I said previously, twice just before his death. When I left I did not have plans for changes as I had a very good job which I liked. I was totally exhausted and most nights came home from school and just crashed. At that time and at other times of serious problems, like surgery, my way of coping was to shut down my feelings, and it worked for me, or so I thought. As a result, my emotional needs were often not met, just ignored over and over again

My faith was, at first, quite black and white. Gradually, my eighteen years of making retreats and workshops at the Cenacle, the course work at Dominican, University of California, and University of San Francisco, general reading, and the changes of Vatican II began making increasingly important changes in my beliefs.

October 5, 2005. It is now some fifty-three years since my first Cenacle retreat. All this time I have, in one way or another, searched to give my life direction and meaning. It is only now that I have clarity about why the various events of my life have been important, one to the other, that I am finding real belonging and peace. This is now evident from the spiritual growth work I have undertaken these last four years. I did not know then how extensively God would use my suffering to help other couples with their marriages. As a Sister, some of the people who came on retreat felt I could understand their dilemma and problems as I had real experience of marriage, the good, and the not so good.

Very shortly after I left Hank I made a retreat at the Cenacle with Msgr. David Rosage of Spokane. He had been involved with the Catholic Charismatic Prayer groups for a short time and gave a retreat entitled Life In The Spirit. As it was the first retreat in our area with that theme, some of us did not know what to expect. The Catholic Charismatic Movement started in Notre Dame, Indiana and had only recently come to the West. At the close of the retreat Msgr. Rosage offered to pray for us to receive the Holy Spirit. I don't remember that I felt anything special but something was certainly rummaging around in the group. Some people talked about special feelings and they seemed highly emotional to me. Two or three people collapsed but didn't know why. A few people started mumbling in what seemed like another language. Some were just silent and seemed deeply touched. I remember we talked about what was happening but at the time few of us really understood what was going on. This first encounter with the Charismatic movement piqued my interest and I decided to seek further information.

Retreatants from San Francisco told me of a prayer group at the University of San Francisco, an easy drive from my Marin apartment. There were about thirty in the group; some priests, a few Sisters, students and others. I found the teachings and the prayer very restful; it was a reflective evening. Though I am not a singer at all

I enjoyed the simple, prayerful music. We broke into small groups of two or three and prayed for each other's needs. A special mass for this group, held on Sunday, saw most of us there; prayer with this group helped meet my spiritual needs as I made my adjustment to single life. I began to be open to a new sense of God and to share spiritual insights with others.

I was free but often my heart was heavy; and I realized I didn't know what I really wanted to do with the rest of my life. Later that same year I moved to San Francisco so that I could take part in more activities there, both at the University of San Francisco and the charismatic prayer group. It was an easy twenty-minute commute to my school from my apartment in the Marina close to the Golden Gate Bridge. During this first year after my separation I kept my sanity by teaching and filling the other hours of the days with music, reading, television, and new friends from the prayer group. I avoided my parents, for Mother asked too many questions. On weekends I sometimes saw my Aunt Hilda and her daughter Roslyn; we would take a drive on Sunday afternoon and have dinner on the way back home, or go away for an overnight stay in Carmel.

That year I took my cousin Roslyn on a Christmas cruise to Mexico. We sailed on Christmas Eve from San Francisco on the *Oriana*, where we had a stateroom in a good location. I remember shopping for my first pantsuit, a beautiful, rather dressy one in navy blue. I didn't get any evening clothes though, as I did not intend to dance. We stopped first at Los Angeles, where Aunt Bunny and Uncle George and others came to visit us. Our next stop was in Puerto Vallarta, then Mazatlan and Acapulco. The weather was beautiful, warm and sunny all day and a great contrast from rainy San Francisco. A large variety of activities were available to passengers. I mostly played duplicate bridge, and just sat in the sun. We took all the tours offered at stops as well as just wandering around in the city centres. When we got to Acapulco one of the men I had met asked me to go to dinner with him, also inviting Roslyn as we had planned to spend time together. We spent the afternoon watching the divers, visiting shops in the older part of town and then went for dinner at the patio of the El Presidente Hotel. Our host was a producer in the movie industry and was on the cruise by himself. He was taking the cruise so as to be away over the holidays, having lost his wife and two children in an accident two years earlier. I must say that the great dinner did not treat me well. I was the only one that got sick; I had Montezuma's Revenge for sure.

The sharp contrast between such a luxury cruise and the poverty in the back streets of our stops made me do some deep soul searching. I had never seen such poverty. I pitied the small boys selling their mothers' wares at the pier and following us up the street. Their merchandise was delicate embroidery and crocheted items, beautiful and cheap; the money they brought was very important to the family yet it was terribly hard to make a sale when there were so many merchants. The children automatically put on a sad face if you turned them down. I wondered what this felt like, so many disappointments day after day.

Another important realization at this time was that the man I met on the ship was quite attracted to me and I to him. We had spent a lot of time together over meals, having cocktails, playing bridge, and just talking. He wanted to come to San Francisco and keep up our relationship. Somehow, this didn't feel right to me. It didn't fit with other experiences I was having. I took it to deep prayer and decided that, while I was attracted, I did not want another intimate relationship with a man.

JOURNEY

steps are unsure
unsung

Much unknown
must be
pathed   experienced

As my
growing
embracing wholeness
continues

Where do I belong? I knew I planned to live my life alone. I now had the opportunity to really dream about what my future would be. I don't know when it came to me, a call to spend my future as a volunteer for a church group. As I mentioned before, when Jean Bo gert died she had left me some money. At my marriage break-up I bought some stocks and other investments. I made good choices, found some great tax write-offs, and quickly made money on the stocks. I felt that putting it all together I could retire and just work for the Lord, whatever that might mean; I would have a modest but assured income.

I had heard good things about Madonna House in Canada but when I found out it was in Ontario I knew I couldn't take the severe winters. I wrote to the Jesuit Volunteers in Washington State and the Frontier Apostles based in Prince George, B.C. As I was trying to decide what to do in the future, I went to the Cenacle. That night I was the only person in the retreat section of the house. I read awhile in the evening, and then tucked into bed for a good sleep. I was suddenly wakened from sleep and, sitting up, observed a huge, strong, white light at the foot of the bed. There was no sound, just the light. Suddenly I heard some words from scripture: "Ask, search, knock and the door will be opened." The words were so clear, slowly said, the light so bright that I was wide awake, and shaking; I stayed that way the rest of the night. I had no one I trusted enough to share my incomprehension of this experience. I didn't have the words, nor did I want anyone to think I was a kook. So I did not share this event with anyone for some years, though it was affirming for me and I did start a real search to find direction for my future.

As I mentioned before, at the prayer group I had met and often talked with one of the nursing Sisters; we were about the same age and both trying to sort out this new Charismatic prayer. My Sister friend came over and listened to all my chatter regarding possible futures. She asked pointed questions and my honest answers all seemed to indicate that I was free to make a choice. The clincher was when she asked me what I would do if I lost all my money, my family refused me help, and I was terribly ill. I said if that remote possibility came up I would probably be too sick to care but that I would then be eligible for care in a veteran's hospital. She said my answer indicated I was free to take a new direction in my life.

Somehow I knew within myself that nothing I was likely to face in future would be any worse than some of my past problems. I had faith in the future, blind faith, as I did not know what it might contain! My angina was in good control so, short of living in the desert or the frozen north, it would not change my openness to call. The children were both grown and self-sustaining. I did not consult either my parents or my children, as I needed to make the choice without any pressure.

I resigned from my job and left the San Francisco Bay Area in 1970. I have only returned on short trips to visit the family. The Superintendent asked me to take a leave of absence, but I knew I didn't need the security of a job and wanted no strings to hamper me in the future. I was happy at Edna Maguire but when I made the decision to leave it was easy to do because there was no shortage of teachers; they could fill my space easily. It was good to be there and good to go. The ten years I taught there had just whizzed by as I enjoyed teaching and found it fulfilling. I had not had a reply from either of the volunteer organizations I had applied to before

195

I made a decision to leave my job; neither the Frontier Apostles nor Jesuit Volunteers had responded.

My financial security allowed me to make the change from employment to volunteer status easily. Working as a volunteer meant that I was choosing simplicity rather than an upper middle class lifestyle. The excitement of two radical changes in my life—no marriage and no job—bolstered me as I chose to deliberately take on this life direction. Heading out I knew not where. Only myself to depend on; scary, yes, but I didn't take time to feel it. I just waited for something to happen.

About three days before I was to leave my apartment a priest from Prince George, British Columbia, called, saying he was in San Francisco and wanted to meet me. He offered me a teaching position in Prince George College, a Frontier Apostle School, at the princely salary of $25.00 per month plus room and board. I decided to give it a try; I had nothing else planned. I looked at a map and realized Prince George was far away. He gave me a list of things I needed, to outfit the car for the trip to the far North. Four days later I drove to Redding, where I got snow tires, and chains that I used as I went up the pass to Ashland, Oregon. I had never driven in snow, but drove in heavy snow the next day up to Hood River, where I stayed over-night. The next day I drove to Spokane through a heavy snowstorm with some white-outs; I did not know the severe danger from the storm. This was scary driving but I kept on and found the Immaculate Heart Retreat house just at noon. The warm welcome moderated my anxiety from the long drive. The trip had exhausted me; I realized I was on automatic pilot. I had left San

Francisco on short notice, and had driven in snow, accompanied only by the car radio and my prayer for a safe journey. The next day I had a block-heater installed so I could plug the car in and keep it from freezing, a must for winter in the North.

At the retreat house I met Sister Dominic from Prince George, who was studying in Spokane; she hinted she would drive up with me if I would pay her airfare back. She didn't drive but a companion would be most welcome as I went north. We set off on a long and tiring journey, stopping near Vancouver B.C., then travelling on to Prince George. We went to Sister Dominic's convent, where I stayed a couple of days. Sister Dominic helped me clean up my dorm room. A pre-war bed with a simple flat wire spring immediately got a sheet of plywood and a five-inch foam mattress, and bedding. Money well spent. The floor was wood and Dominic scrubbed it while I went out to get a rug to place by my bed. The room was heated by a primitive oil stove so I was glad to have some warm blankets. A major, major change in my entire life style within just six days! Living in a disaster of a barracks room, several feet of snow pushed into banks outside, with fresh snow every day. The cold reached to minus 40C even during the day. Sometimes I wondered if I had lost my mind and decided maybe it was just frozen.

I taught Native students in the high school, a strikingly different challenge. My subjects were remedial reading and math and several classes of cooking. The well-equipped kitchen had no supplies; the school had spent the budget for the year. I just used my own money and took the girls shopping at Safeway. They knew little about what was available or how to shop, so we had some very informative sessions. My classes prepared and served a special buffet dinner for seventy-five people. We had moose stew, vegetable salad, roasted potato wedges, and Nanaimo bars for dessert. It was some job getting it all done; my students were justly proud of their efforts and every bit of food disappeared pronto. There was a real challenge in the remedial classes. The students were interested in getting an education and had quite good follow-through. This new kind of teaching was rewarding because, when these older students started getting the hang of math or reading, they just charged ahead; success was a great encourager.

One of the girls invited me to their reservation to a special Long House ceremony where Bishop O'Grady celebrated Mass wearing his deerskin-beaded vestments. Native dancing and drumming preceded dinner. I never saw so many ways of cooking moose, elk, and chicken. Pasta dishes and salads finished off the meal. Several of the Sisters from town enjoyed the day too.

Over the months I got to know the Mercy Sisters, who were from Ireland. On many a Saturday or Sunday we would fill the car and go off to some remote Indian Mission School, where their Sisters taught, taking the food with us and cooking it there. It was a new experience to be with Sisters as an equal. There were two people about my age on staff, one a former secretary to the Cardinal of Los Angeles and the other a Sister of Charity from Vancouver who taught shop. We thought nothing of driving fifty or sixty miles for lunch on a weekend, and one time we went all the way to

Jasper. I was the only one who had a car and it was well equipped for any and all weather conditions.

There were fishing lakes close to Prince George, and if one wore long-sleeved shirts and lathered on mosquito lotion, it was possible to catch good fish. One day I went fishing with Mac. She was slow getting out her gear so I went eagerly ahead down to the lakeside. I threw in my line and immediately caught a huge fish. It started struggling to get to the weeds. I yelled at Mac to bring the net quickly as it was all I could do to hold the fish. It was too difficult to walk down the bank to where there was a better place to play him. In any case she got there in time and I netted a twenty-inch brown trout. I took it back to the barracks, baked it and we all enjoyed the catch. One weekend Mac and I went out into the real wild near Fort St. John to camp. We just threw our sleeping bags on the ground, as we had no tent, only a small tarp to give us some protection from the cold ground. It was breathtakingly beautiful to lie there and see the Northern Lights. It was a spectacular show and one I will never forget. I have seen the lights a couple of times from here on Vancouver Island but nothing like that show. We nearly froze to death, but it was fun.

Prince George College offered me another contract but I turned it down. I loved the school and students and knew I would miss the challenge but the weather was just too harsh for me. As a result of the months in Prince George I was now certain my call was to serve others. I knew that this kind of life, the slower pace, working for room and board, was both satisfying to me and helpful to others. It certainly was teaching in a very different way and the poverty of teaching materials called on all my creativity to meet the needs of the students. All the schools in the Diocese of Prince George, were staffed with teachers who received room and board and tiny stipends. The teaching staff was made up of youngsters just out of college, or retired teachers like me. All of us were trying to do a bit to help sustain the missionary work in the north.

When I left Prince George in August I did not know where I would be settling, so I left some of my things at the convent. Mac and I drove from Prince George to Prince Rupert on the coast; a beautiful drive. We stayed overnight at a convent there. The next morning we took the ferry and after an overnight cruise down the Inner Passage, landed near Port Hardy. From there it was a five-hour drive to Nanaimo, where we got the ferry across to Vancouver. I enjoyed this carefree life and I was sure something else would turn up for me. This sojourn of some ten months in Prince George came as a gift when I was ready to leave San Francisco seeking a new vocation.

REFLECT

Alone
unique…
my path crosses Yours

reflection
relationship

marking
placing a stepping stone

for me
or someone else
following God's way

✠

I decided to head to Spokane for a few days' rest, and
to see where Our Lord would lead me next. "Stop here
and work for us" was the offer of Msgr. Rosage. I took
the job, at $50 per month plus room and board—dou-
ble my last salary. As I learned the ropes, I did everything from secretarial work to cooking to retreat direction. Early in the fall Sister Dominic and I drove back
to Prince George to gather my possessions. We made it
into a fun trip, stopping overnight at 100 Mile House
in both directions. Really a long drive that weekend,
but we enjoyed the fall colours, the animals coming
down for better pasture, and the brief visit with the
Mercy Sisters.

To supplement my religion classes from Dominican
I decided to go to Gonzaga, in Spokane, and took Old
and New Testament from Father Armand Nigro, S.J.,
as well as classes from other professors. Father Nigro
was an excellent teacher and showed the classes slides
he had taken in Israel. When Nigro and other Jesuits started to train retreat directors, I took those classes as well. Those of us on the retreat staff often went

to the special liturgies held for the priests and Sisters at Gonzaga. This was an extraordinary time of new church life for many Catholics and it was wonderful to have so many opportunities to experience the changes. I went to one of the first communal penance services which were just beginning. A gathering hymn, a brief prayer, and a short teaching was followed by a period of quiet reflection. The service concluded with a prayer of forgiveness and absolution. All of the liturgical services, including the Eucharist, were in English.

There was a very active Charismatic prayer group at the Retreat House as well as a group of priests and Sisters at Gonzaga. Sometimes members of the retreat house staff attended prayer meetings in the nearby areas to give support to those just starting up. At a group in the small town of Wallace, Idaho we were praying and someone said, "There has been a healing in the group". All of us were silent. Suddenly I found words coming out of my mouth, "I have had a healing of my heart condition." It was a shock to hear myself saying those words for I didn't know where they came from. I shook to the core, trembling all over and was totally bewildered; the whole group was startled. I felt as if I didn't know myself. I was different but could not say just how. I didn't know when my heart was healed, just knew it was some time in the very recent past. Surely the strangest feeling I ever encountered. Other people were excited and asked many questions, it was hard for me to answer; I just wanted to be quiet and let the experience soak in. It took a while for me to feel I was able to drive home safely.

The angina since my mid-thirties had kept me on medication and I took nitro-glycerine as needed. Later that day I realized that I had not taken any nitro for quite a while. Bewildered, I got myself to a heart specialist who checked me, reviewed the previous EKG's from California, and said my angina seemed cured as I had a normal cardiogram. He stopped all my medications and said I was as good as new. I felt like it too. I had no trouble believing him because the awareness of the healing had already given me the news of the change within my heart. It still took a few more weeks for me to realize that some previously closed doors were now open. I re-learned to run and play and do many more physical activities than I had previously. Most important, I was no longer afraid.

November 2004. Reflecting back over the years I know that part of the healing was physical. The stress of my marriage and the leave-taking were gone. Living at a totally different, slower pace no doubt contributed to the change in my physical condition. I began to live my life taking no precautions about my heart. The best part of the healing was that I had completely lost my fear of my heart disease. A miracle to be sure.

Yes, the angina returned some years later. I had gone to the doctor to have a check-up and he said everything, including the cardiogram was normal. Just a few days later I was in the main lounge at Shalom, upset about something and I realized that my abdomen felt weird, with pain, pressure, and general discomfort that took several minutes to go away. I scheduled another doctor's appointment and he listened to my story. His diagnosis, after another EKG, was that the angina had returned and he gave me medicine specifically for angina that was not available at the onset of my first symptoms. The Beta blocker controls my angina and I have only taken nitro-glycerine a very few times in the last twenty years. I have had several hospitalizations for arrhythmia, have had a pacemaker since 1999, and have had several rather serious bouts of heart failure. In spite of all this, the anxiety and fears of earlier days are completely gone. A great relief.

My second year in Spokane the Jesuits and Monsignor Rosage gave a thirty-day retreat/workshop for those interested in spiritual direction. Father Nigro invited me to participate. Like scripture classes, this retreat seemed a natural addition to prepare myself for whatever the Lord planned for my future. It was there that I met Sister Jean Ann Berning, a Benedictine sister from Mt. Angel, Oregon. We were drawn to each other so, as I had my car, we would be off and about on break days. We spent many hours talking about our lives and, in my case, about the fact that I had no plans for the future. Jean Ann had already thought of going to Canada to start a daughter house there, and was planning to seek permission at their annual community meeting in late summer. She invited me to visit her in Mt. Angel, which I did one weekend in May.

Jean Ann took me to visit the infirmary, which was impressive because of the way all the Sisters of the community were able to share in the lives of the elderly, making them an active part of community life, attending the spiritual exercises as they were able. A deep care was evident. The busy workers were obviously keeping the infirm Sisters up on the latest news, just as one would expect in a family where several generations lived under one roof.

By late fall of 1972 I had been on the road for about two years, first in Prince George and then in Spokane. The call that started in January 1970 pointed me to work for the Lord and I had found it rewarding. I never once thought of returning to the Bay Area, or to any of my previous professional work. I was becoming more certain that my future life and work would be as a volunteer for the church. I went to live with the Good Shepherd Sisters in Spokane and was there for about three months, discerning my direction. It became apparent that it was not with the Good Shepherds, as they were in some turmoil about the direction the order might take. Nearly all the Sisters under forty had just left, part of the exodus all convents were facing in this post-Vatican II era. Many people had ideas of what I might do in the future; Father Nigro wanted me to buy a house in Spokane and operate it for Sisters who were attending Gonzaga and needed a place to stay. Some Sisters thinking of leaving religious life needed a halfway house. Neither of these works appealed to me.

Next, I spent three weeks at an Indian Mission replacing the cook; seventy-five for lunch and twelve for breakfast and dinner. I did not want this as a permanent job for sure. After I returned from the cooking stint in Idaho I chose to camp out in a public park in Spokane for a couple of weeks. It was a fairly large park, well maintained and equipped with hot showers. I fitted out my small yellow VW station wagon with the mattress I had purchased in Prince George. I could sleep in the car quite comfortably by pushing some of my belongings aside and stacking up others to make room. I had my Coleman stove and a small ice chest. It was a beautiful early fall and I was quite comfortable and felt safe. I could easily have gone to a motel or stayed at the retreat house but being by myself in this kind of situation drew me. A rather unusual place for a temporary home but I was just waiting for something to point the way.

Sister Jean Ann kept in touch and told me in September of an opening for a parish social worker in Silverton, Oregon. I certainly didn't have a degree in that area but she thought I would qualify based on my life experiences and former education. I drove down to Oregon to see about it. Jean Ann really has caught Benedict's admonition to treat any guest as if they were Christ. I had no suspicion of her true agenda, yet Jean Ann presented religious life so invitingly that she enticed me to take a look at her way of life as I decided on my future. I was not a typical invitee because of my age and status in the church as a married woman. Jean Ann was directly involved in my opening myself to a vowed life, and later influenced me again when she accepted my offer to go to Nanaimo for a year. Little did any of us realize I would ultimately become a member of the community and make Nanaimo my permanent home.

COME

Called forth loved daughter
always with you
I will teach you all you need to know

come follow Me loved daughter
you belong to Me
come with Me… be with Me
walk, run and play

always with you
give you breath…
life…strength…soul

Come, I lead the way
you know not the places still to see
come   let go   :
just be with Me always

March 2005. As I looked into my journals, this
vagabond era was coming to a close. The classes
in Spokane, the work at the retreat house and my
prayer were all preparation for a new undertaking. My prayer and reading were a gathering of
information, not a sense of Presence in my call,
but a sure direction and I seemed to know that
heading to Mt. Angel for a parish job was my next

step. The step was a far deeper one than I could possibly have imagined. I found myself taking off, once again trusting in the accuracy of my call. I was at peace.

MT. ANGEL: HOME

I arrived at Queen of Angels Monastery during the hour of Evening Prayer, Vespers; no one answered the door so I went across the street to the Angels Table and had a burger. I had driven from Spokane to investigate a job in a local parish; perhaps another way to serve as a volunteer. Sister Jean Ann invited me to stay at the convent while I was making my decision. I was also attending community prayer and meals. As a result of Vatican II, some religious communities were breaking into small prayer groups where they shared dreams, fears, and anticipations regarding the future of community. Jean Ann invited me to Shalom, a group of about ten Sisters who met weekly for spiritual sharing and mutual support. The evening was an introduction to how deeply and uniquely changes had affected these women. It was the birthday of one of the Sisters and we had coffee and cake at the end of the meeting. Sister Eileen's input interested me, so we stayed for about an hour to finish our conversation. A soft-spoken, thoughtful, rather shy woman about seven years younger than I, Eileen entered religious life directly from high school; she had been educated at Mt. Angel College and had her Master's degree from one of the State colleges. She had always been a teacher and at this time taught First Grade, her favourite age group, at the local public school.

I was attracted to her by her gentle manner, particularly as she spoke about prayer and her experience of some of the new changes. Grounded in her faith, she spoke of it as the source of her life force. Eileen told me of her relationship with a loving God who guided her from her earliest days; while still very young she knew when she finished high school that she would move the few blocks to the convent and begin her life's work there. I was hearing a story a far cry from my own disastrous relationship with God. I had lived with and alongside individual Sisters and priests but this was my introduction into religious community life. As I experienced the daily rhythm of convent life and prayer, I felt compelled to explore entering religious life. Honestly, I do not know when it came to me that I might ask to join the community. In my usual way I quietly mulled this over for several days.

I arranged an appointment with Sister Antoinette Traeger, Prioress, and asked if she would consider my entering the community. Knowing the challenges sure to come because of my age and life experiences, she felt it was appropriate to test my vocation and gave me her approval to enter. Neither of us knew if I could get

Canonical permission, but I could become a Postulant. I had not even an inkling of what it would be like to live life as a vowed religious. I just stepped out and started to live the life. I had to do it that way as I didn't even know the questions to ask, but knew they would come quickly. I flew to California for ten days to see my children and parents and to tell them personally of my decision to enter the Benedictines. My mother was aghast; Dad made no comment.

The Benedictine Order, founded in the fifth century in Italy, is the oldest and largest religious order in the Catholic Church. Benedictines are monastics, living under a Rule and an Abbot or Prioress, and their specific work is prayer. Each monastery or Abbey is an independent community responsible for its way of living out the Rule, with a relationship to other Benedictine monasteries in their area. Sisters came from Maria Rickenbach in Switzerland to found Queen of Angels Monastery in Mt. Angel in 1882. When I entered in 1972, there were 119 Sisters in community. Ten years had passed since the advent of Vatican II and it was immediately evident that religious houses were all in a state of change. Mass and the Liturgy of the Hours were already in English. The Community prayed in the large chapel but a small group had difficulty with the liturgical changes so continued to use the prayer books of old, praying in St. Joseph's Chapel.

When I entered the formation program that fall, each postulant had an individual director; Sister Eileen Kraemer was mine. We met weekly for discussion of the basics of community living, study, sharing on the Rule of Benedict, and other assigned spiritual reading.

I also took classes at the Mt. Angel Seminary just up the hill and worked part-time at the Silverton Parish.

I wanted what Eileen had, a deeply spiritual life, exemplified by her priorities of daily prayer, and presence in community activities; in every way she was an excellent mentor. She was quite encouraging, always answered my endless questions, and was not shocked by some of my past. We began to share free time, often out in the woods observing God's creation. Around Mt. Angel, like on the ranch, there were hidden treasures, and silence to quiet the soul, which helped me find stability in the midst of change.

Both Eileen and I were grappling with change; she, with acceptance of new prayer forms and a call to more active participation with adults; I, of course, was searching for a meaningful and sustaining relationship with God and a new way of service for life. To this day, my relationship with God continues to be my primary goal; I am always searching, deepening, expanding, and demanding more connection to my God.

As I have worked on my story, I still do not know just how I could have entered religious life, embraced a structured environment, and given up at least part of my self-direction of the past two years. I never knew if I would succeed in living the life as many of its demands were hard to follow, yet no one ever asked me to leave. I lived my days one by one, could not even anticipate what might cloud the future. I soon learned of the struggle of others whose own journey on a slightly different path helped to make a community of strong women who could willingly face an unknown future. Benedictines take a vow of stability, which means living in the same monastery for life. This is a stable force for many who are in pain, who wobble, and need support and prayer to help them find peace in time of trial. Living in the same monastery for life also makes you face the fact that your faults and strengths are seen by those who live their lives side by side with you, and there is no place to run. Growth and conversion are challenges for all.

The daily life of a religious, previously so predictable, now included change in prayer times, talking at meals, and even the newest postulant went to the evening gatherings in the Community Room. When I entered Mt. Angel the daily schedule was as follows:

Rising bell 5:30
Morning Prayer at 6:30 followed by Eucharist
Breakfast
Private Prayer or Lectio Divina using scripture
Classes or work, in my case in Silverton
Noon Prayer followed by lunch
Afternoon of work or classes
Vespers 5:30
Supper
Recreation in community room
Compline 7:30
Grand silence until morning bell

While this schedule structured the day, many people varied from this basic outline. For example, Eileen left after breakfast to go downtown to teach her First Grade students, always wearing lay clothes, as she taught in public school. Her own personal prayer and classes

213

with me took place after her return from school. In my own case, I usually left after breakfast to work in the Silverton Parish, some days returning at noon, others spending part of the afternoon visiting parishioners. I felt at ease with this schedule; it was a busy one, but then all my life I had filled my hours with activity. I loved the prayer in chapel and did not find any of the schedules difficult. On weekends there was free time in the afternoons, which I often spent out in the wilds.

Some of the Sisters were avid card players and one evening I offered to play. Sister Perpetua and others liked my card skills and began to downplay some of my differences from the usual postulant. When we played games or just chatted, they were full of stories, for some had been in community nearly seventy years. I learned community history, about the tremendous sacrifices willingly made, deprivations during the Depression and of hidden pain and suffering just accepted as part of community life. One of the major messages was, "God will provide."

It was the older sisters who readily spoke about their hardships who helped verify my call to religious life, that this was the right place for me, and who gave me courage to persevere. By the time I got there, Sister Flavia was in an electric wheelchair. She was quite limited physically but was a great card player and a greater storyteller. She came to one of the Houses of Prayer and spoke to the sisters about her call, telling us how her father had walked her to the Convent and had her trunk sent by dray. Sister Imelda also was in a wheelchair. She had lots of wisdom to impart. More than once she said, "It will happen when it is time." She knew how hard some of the changes were for me, and that making a transition from an independent life of many years to a community sister would not be an easy task.

Sister Perpetua, in her eighties, was a good model for me; she entered from Switzerland and never returned even for a visit. She was still a bit peppery; she had lived through all kinds of spiritual and community difficulties and her clear faith in God's will and direction has helped me in my entire religious life. Her example of softening as she aged has been an excellent guide as it has given me hope of change as I grow into my own final years. The prayer in Chapel, the quiet, helped me make the transition, especially when I encountered so many new do's and don'ts at once, and some of those even changed day by day. Frankly, some of the admonitions never made any kind of sense to me, they were just something to accept. If one is looking for logic, a religious life is not the place to find it.

During my first year at Mt. Angel I worked part-time in the Silverton Parish as a social worker. I worked with parishioners who might have need for financial or other help and referred them to appropriate agencies. I also made family visits to take a kind of census and to see how the parish might serve them better.

The first heavy snow of December 1972 called me to drive out and take pictures, as the snow had stopped and the sky was clear. Trees, bushes, and fields were especially beautiful with their thick coats of snow glistening in the bright sun. Eileen and I drove up a hill to Silver Creek Falls; the traffic was light, the snow deep, the snow plough had cleared only one lane. Just then a dump truck crested the hill and started down directly toward us, and in our path, the only path. There was nowhere to go. An inner voice told me to keep going. My insides quivered, I can still recall the feeling, yet somehow I knew we would be safe. This was an overwhelmingly clear knowledge and as the truck came barrelling down toward us an intense white light came between our small yellow VW van and the truck; God's cushion of safety. We passed. I stopped the car and shook and tried to breathe; it took awhile for me to get my breath, as it did Eileen. A gift of life, a call to go on.

All Sisters shared community chores and the first summer I took part in several community canning parties. We sat in the long hall directly opposite the fruit kitchen and peeled fruit or vegetables. Kernels of community life, stories of the old days, were frequent topics of conversation as we sat together. Sister Bernarda, our farmer, saw how fast I worked and took me into the fruit kitchen to bottle the fruit, fitting peaches into jars, just as I had learned at Grandma's knee.

When I entered Mt. Angel I felt the same as when I entered marriage, you give it your best. Commitment! There was a long time for evaluation, but the call I heard demanded trying with everything at my disposal. And I did. Dedication did not make it easier but was helpful when it came to staying power. I learned from my marriage that I would really need to put conscious effort into making it work and keep open to growth opportunities. Of course, I was in a relationship to many more people than in a marriage, but some of the same demands for openness, listening, and growth presented themselves. The transition to community life will always be difficult for older women. Several women entered during my early years, stayed a time and left. In my novitiate and years as a Junior Sister I took a number of courses at the Mt. Angel Abbey such as Psalms, Benedictine History, The Holy Rule, and Moral Theology, but the class that helped me most was Pastoral Counselling, given by a psychiatrist in Portland. I spent at least an hour a day in private prayer and another in spiritual reading or Lectio.

In the last part of my Novitiate Sister Eileen and I set up a two-week House of Prayer Experience. Sisters attending summer session at the Mt. Angel Seminary could elect to do the House of Prayer. It was part of my job to set up the space, select the presenter, cook the meals, and generally see that things went well. We had ten retreatants and hired a monk who had been highly recommended. Disaster struck. After two presentations all of us decided Father's conferences were less than adequate. Eileen and I worked round the clock to prepare the material we needed for prayer and conferences. We rescued the retreat!

I did not find it easy to start retreat work even though I was technically prepared, as I stuck out as a newcomer. At both Immaculate Heart Retreat and at Gonzaga I took classes and worked in supervised Spiritual Direction and hoped someday I could minister in that area.

June 2002. Retreat work has been just right for me, and for many other sisters. By running a retreat center we offer a safe place for others to come where they can separate from their daily routine and spend time listening and reflecting. Some come wanting to listen to and embrace the pain or new events in their lives. It is also a time when people can reflect on how changes might strengthen their direction in life, particularly opening new areas for growth and leaving some of the overused methods of the past behind. Retreats can and do often offer new insights of what could be... if we will only discipline ourselves to hear and to find the new. Workshops, Scripture, music, reading, sharing with a director, are all ways one uses retreat time; it is entirely up to the retreatant. Most retreat centers offer specialized workshops or speakers on spiritual topics.

I have always been an instigator of something new. A builder, I seem to have a mental picture and a sense of how something can happen, be it a change in direction, a new value as a guide, space renovated and put to a different use, or starting a program that will better meet the needs of others. Curiosity, unlimited vision, and heightened awareness have been gifts I have used all my life. Perhaps some people would say I bring about too much change. And perhaps I do, as I always look for a more effective way. Change, not for its own sake, but to make life easier has brought criticism from co-workers who are less open to what new things might be just around the corner. I like to take a peek! This is not a usual gift found in religious who are used to saying, "We have always done it this way." Change comes slowly. I remember one of the sisters giving me minute instructions on how to set a table for Thanksgiving—placement of glasses, silverware, napkins etc.; I wondered at the time what she thought I had been doing for the past thirty or more years.

Coming from a different past life has made it easy for me to start something new. My particular focus at that time was to make Shalom Prayer Center a viable entity. Gradually, I felt more comfortable. In 1976 we took over half of the second floor in the Education Building. My energy has always been boundless and somehow I attract volunteer helpers who also take on extra work. We had a contractor who did the basic renovations, but volunteers did all the painting and put together the new furniture. Over fifteen beds, desks, and nightstands were needed for our new rooms. My work experiences of the last thirty years were not typical of a Sister. My history shows I have good administrative ability, can focus, and run an office and still be creative.

We soon added some evening programs and started a Charismatic prayer group. Father Charles Harris from Notre Dame, Indiana, a Chaplain at the University of Oregon, one of the first priests involved in the Charismatic Renewal, ran several prayer groups in the area. He was a presenter at one of the two-week summer sessions and then helped Sister Eileen and me as we set up a prayer group at Shalom. Sister Eileen continued with her teaching in Mt. Angel and helped at Shalom evenings, weekends and in the summer.

I made first vows on December 21, 1974, not having guests because of the Christmas season, and the distance from my family. Reading my vows before the community was indeed an awesome experience. I meant every word of them, knowing that living out the vows called for day-by-day commitment to prayer and growth. I found myself at age fifty vowing to lead a life that invited change, that required me to make challenging transitions, and necessitated at least three or four more years before final acceptance. Many of my former life skills—for example, just get the problem solved and move on—were of little use or deemed inappropriate. I often found myself impatient with the pace of community decisions. The community way of checking things out piece by piece was hard, for often one suggested solution was not better than another, and all were slow. An interesting aside is that I tried to change the name from Education Building to Shalom Prayer Center. The majority of community would not go along with it, saying, "It's always been the Education Building and it was part of the Mt. Angel College Campus." By the time I joined the community, the College was on the way out, and a prayer center started; today, many years later, the whole building is now for Shalom's use and is so named.

On many Sunday afternoons and during the long evenings of summer, Eileen and I would go off so I could take pictures. We would walk in the forest, spot something interesting and I would take a picture or two. One day, walking down a logging road near Scotts Mills we spotted a mushroom with a drop of moisture about to fall off. Down went a garbage sack and I positioned myself flat on the ground so I could study the mushroom and get the perfect shot. Eileen tried to hurry me for some reason, probably because it was time to go back, but I kept my focus, it was not a time to be rushed. To this day, it is one of my two best pictures; even Eileen thinks so as she has a big enlarged version of it in her office. This getting back to nature was a respite from all the newness of community life; a welcomed opportunity to relate to the wonders of nature. Sometimes when I spotted an unusual flower, leaf, or moss on a log, the find seemed to speak to me, putting words to what I saw. One needs to take a picture the minute it is presented; coming back even a few minutes later changes the light or makes the voice just different enough so that the special beauty is gone.

Living so near forests and the sea gave me many opportunities for taking outstanding pictures which I used to make slide shows, using psalms or my own text, and music to get a message across. I made many sets of such meditations, including several videotapes. The combination of eye/word as seen in nature seemed ever before me and in taking a photo, I often knew exactly where and how I would use it to illustrate a point or theme. One fall day, while walking along on a leaf-strewn path, I stopped suddenly, my eye drawn to a decaying leaf. It was a large maple leaf, its colour bleached by the sun, and death well underway as evidenced by its surface holes. The dying process had formed it into a pyramid shaped tent. Immediately I stopped, got in the best light, and took a few shots; I called it "The Tent of God".

Once when we were at the coast we went down a small dead end road near Glenden Beach. We found a very small pond with a bit of running water, lots of foliage, five finger ferns, and one yellow skunk cabbage. We spent a lot of time there and were nearly ready to go when I went for the last shot. Well, I got the shot but I also was stuck up above my knee in slimy goo.

It was quite difficult to extricate myself, let alone my boot. This was more than twenty-five years ago. When going by that area a couple of years ago we stopped to see what had changed. The pond was all filled in and the special features were now totally gone. But, not so my picture, the one in my mind or the one in my slide collection.

A bit of music, a hymn or a psalm might open my mind to a thought or to words that came with such strength that I needed to write them down. This kind of insight happened to me quite frequently, so I kept a paper and pencil on the pew shelf where I sat for office. I had found that waiting until prayer was over meant I usually lost the words. Sister Perpetua had asked me to sit in her pew and soon noted that I wrote sometimes in the midst of prayer. However, when I explained what and why I was scribbling, she blessed my work.

Shalom kept me busy for the next several years as we expanded the offerings, worked with individual retreatants, and hosted groups bringing their own programs. I continued to do most of the cooking and Eileen started working full time at Shalom. For over twenty-five years I had made personal retreats and attended many spiritual workshops, usually at the Cenacle, and had experience also at Immaculate Heart in Spokane.

These experiences made me aware of what was of interest to people and helped as we set up our programs. We started with a First Friday Day of Recollection for local women. We gathered in the chapel for morning prayer, followed by a short conference, then some time for quiet reflection followed by Mass and lunch. The afternoon schedule had another short conference followed by reflection time, and group sharing. Attendance was consistently good. The prayer group enlarged and many men and women came on Wednesday mornings and some stayed into the afternoon. My skill as a soup cook came into use as, on Wednesday, I would use all the leftovers from the weekend. One could never anticipate the kind of soup, but sharing it made for a congenial group over a lunch bowl. Father Harris helped us to start the Inner Healing Retreats that we gave for many years. We also invited Retreat Masters such as Father Armand Nigro, Dr. Thomas Francoeur, Father Ted Dobson, who initiated us in Enneagrams, and others who facilitated Journaling retreats, and couples' weekends. We tried to have programs that would help us deepen our faith and broaden our spiritual life. We were busy nearly every weekend, particularly after we had fifteen bedrooms available.

Sometimes Eileen and I would go out into the wild overnight, taking our gear with us, which consisted of two sleeping bags, matches, a pot or two, bare food necessities and of course, paper, pencil and camera. Over the years, we traveled through Western Canada on several occasions, as well as Washington and Oregon, and down the coast to visit my parents near Santa Rosa. The special beauty of the parks including Zion, Yosemite, Big Trees, Grand Canyon, Yellowstone, and Monument Valley thrilled us. I remember that it was cold in Monument Valley in late August and we stretched our sleeping bags out in the back of the van. My agenda was to take sunrise pictures at a certain spot; I tried to wake Eileen but she was sleepy so I drove off and she continued sleeping in the back. A few bumps and she was wide awake. I did get special pictures. I have no favourite vacations or trips, as all are different and all bring to mind wonderful memories with pictures to prove it. We couldn't afford motels, but got along well as campers, even though we had no tent.

August 2004. Exploring in nature put me in touch with many of my childhood questions that had no answers; scientists are only now understanding these phenomena and passing the answers along. Over the years, the special insights of nature obviously related more and more to my spirituality. I found wonder all over the earth, around each corner or under a leaf or growing on the top of a mother log in a rain forest. I am so grateful to God for my ranch and the eye- and mind-openers that have always been a part of my life. I sensed the circle of life and death as I experienced the seasons of the year and the life-span of trees and other forest finds. My curiosity led me to question how and why plants grew. One day, when I was still a small child walking in the meadow, I saw a shoot pushing up through the earth, and a day or so later it had burst into bloom; not tended, as Mother tended her plants in her garden. Something different and unknown was happening before my very eyes. It took a lifetime to find answers to some of the questions I asked early on, some of which I am asking still.

✠

In 1976, Sister Eileen celebrated twenty-five years in religious life. As a special treat she wanted to go to Europe with me. It was time to use the travel money Jean Bogart had left me. With some trepidation we asked Sister Antoinette for the necessary permissions; I was quite surprised when we got approval.

Eileen was still teaching so I made all our arrangements. Our itinerary was as follows: Portland to New York, overnight, Israel for ten days, Amsterdam, then by car for some weeks, leaving the car in Brussels and travelling by train to Paris; to Dover by boat-train, drive a few weeks, return to London and head for home. Quite a project! It was relatively easy to gather the background materials and make a rough estimate of timing and costs. Eileen got permission to end her teaching year a couple of weeks early, so we took off on May 15th, my birthday. After our brief tour of New York we found our late afternoon El Al flight cancelled, so they put us on a Swiss Air flight leaving immediately. We landed in Zurich, then flew on to Israel.

Next morning we got our blue Volkswagen Bug and found our way to the Old City. Cultural shock set in. At Damascus Gate an uprising brought soldiers who told us to leave. We re-parked at Herod's Gate, but got a shouted message from an Arab merchant that we were in a dangerous area. We left exploring the Old City for another day. We found our way to Bethlehem University where Sisters of the Holy Name had arranged rooms for us in a local convent. We were terribly tired so we

225

found a small shop on the main square of Bethlehem selling shawarma, which is aromatically seasoned lamb roasted on a vertical rotisserie and sliced off, put into a pita, topped with onions, tomato, cucumbers, lettuce, and yogurt sauce. This plus a Coke cost just two US dollars. This kind of food became a mainstay of our diet.

A loud, haunting call at 5:00 AM caused us both to bolt out of our rooms, wide-awake. We gradually relaxed as we identified it as the Moslem's call to prayer, to praise Allah. Sleep was over for us so we dressed and went immediately to the Basilica where we attended a Greek Orthodox Mass in the crypt. The tradition at the Orthodox Mass is to share the bread with all who are there, and thus this special bread was my first liturgical sharing in Israel. At the end of this service the Roman Catholic priest entered and said Mass at the small altar attended by about five of us. A truly unique experience!

Each morning after breakfast we went to Jerusalem. We visited all the Holy City going to Mass in a wide variety of churches. At the Holy Sepulchre there were masses of pilgrims all talking at once and the discourtesy shown to these holy spots made it difficult to pray there, yet it was an experience we wouldn't have wanted to miss.

Driving from Bethlehem to Hebron most of the Palestinians were quite friendly and the workers in the vineyards and fields let us take pictures of them and their work. Looking up to a hill across the highway we saw two large groups of men and women yelling and fighting, with some of the participants bending down to pick up stones and throw them at the others. Stoning for real! I tried to photograph it but someone observed me, yelled and shook fists at me, and others then saw us as well. A few men started down the hillside to make us stop, so I dove for the car, gunned it, and left the scene. This event told me that in some ways not much had changed in inter-relationships since the time of Jesus.

We took off across Samaria for Nazareth where Mary's Well, the only water source in Nazareth, was still in use, with women carrying water jars on their head. We visited the Basilica, St. Joseph's Church and of course the Arab markets. Unless you have seen and smelled the rankness of the meat markets you can't believe them. Each morning the butcher slaughters the lamb, skins it, and hangs the carcass on a hook on the wall. The butcher cuts off any piece you wish, leaving the rest hanging for another shopper. Live chickens are caged or tied by the market stalls, waiting for a customer. Men call out their wares, attracting customers. An unforgettable experience! During all our time there we assuaged our hunger by eating lamb or falafel—highly seasoned ground chick pea balls cooked in hot oil—fresh fruits, and drinking bottled water. The Arab market had many bakeries and we sampled pita bread and many of the honey-flavoured desserts.

My driving skills came to good use as we took our blue VW up the switchback road to the top of Mt. Tabor, the traditional site of the Transfiguration, where we looked out over the beautiful orchards and vegetable fields of the Jezreel Valley. All this area used to be swampy and full of mosquitos. In recent years the

Israelis drained the swamps, reclaimed and tilled the soil, and now produce vegetables and fruits that are for sale not only in Israel but are also shipped out to Europe. Getting down from Tabor is something else, for the road is narrow, the cliffs plunge straight down and many hold their breath at a turn. Several years later, when leading my first tour group, I found the bus had to park part-way up and we had to finish our journey by taxi. Coming down, the taxis whipped around the corners and thrilled, or panicked, many of my tour group.

We stopped in Cana and Naim on our way to the Galilee where we visited the Church of the Beatitudes, Capernaum, the Benedictine Loaves and Fishes church, and other sites. This is the area where many of the parables took place, among them the Sower and the Seed, and the Feeding of Five Thousand. It was wonderful to look out over the Sea of Galilee across only a very few building sites; mostly the eye caught the brown hills, and the blue sea with a few small boats.

Our exploration of the Galilee and other areas certainly verified all I had heard or read about the Holy Land. The hills were barren with green patches where springs were evident, and groves of olive, banana, and citrus trees clustered along the north end of the lake. Villages were tiny and obviously old. All buildings, large or small, old or new were made of the same white sandstone. Open fields, little traffic, small Arab or Israeli villages, are common in the Galilee and I was impressed by the simplicity of the places where Jesus walked and taught and died. Nazareth, at least the old part of it, is a small Arab city, site of the large Roman

Catholic Basilica of the Annunciation. In Tiberius they were just starting to build tourist hotels; Ein Giv and two other kibbutzes are on the lake front. The road around the Sea of Galilee is close to the shore, so one can see fishing boats cast their nets. We stopped at one of the kibbutzes one evening and watched a fisherman just at the edge of the weeds; he used a rubber plunger to make a noise and vibration in the water, directing more fish into his net.

We continued down alongside the Jordan to Jericho, Qumran, the Dead Sea and then back to Jerusalem. Wild yellow daisies carpeted many of the hillsides and an occasional small town and a flock of sheep passed into our view. One of the things that struck me about Israel was how small it is. Bethlehem and Jerusalem are only six miles apart and the Galilee only about four hours north. Except for Jerusalem, all the towns of biblical times are quite small; some, of course, are limited to archaeological sites.

Walking along the shore of the Sea of Galilee, or in areas of Jerusalem, one can get a real sense of what it must have been like during the time of Jesus because the topography hasn't changed much. One is rarely able to pinpoint the exact spot where something took place and that only makes the general sense of the land of Jesus more meaningful. Pilgrims walking down from Bethpage to Jerusalem, as Jesus did on Palm Sunday, may be walking some fifty yards away from the actual path; the feeling of the walk and the vision of the city is the same. Both Eileen and I found that we fell into prayer easily at the various sites, especially along the Sea of Galilee, as we stopped several times as we circled it. We always took time for personal prayer when we visited the sites and often walked up to where we had an outlook over the whole area. I was filled with awe at the time of the trip, and this sense of peace and presence as one walks on this ground has stayed with me ever since. Scripture came alive in a new way. My prayer has changed too, but more about that later.

October 2005. I have a good imagination and a favourite prayer I use when in trouble. I use my memory and imagination to pick out a lonely site along the shore of the Sea of Galilee. One can really be alone and I imagine, as I walk along, that the person just in front of me is Jesus; he too is slowly walking along the shore. Gradually I catch up with him; I cannot see his face, because of a head scarf, but deep within, I know it is He. I say out my thoughts, express my feelings, my needs. I do not receive an answer in words, yet we silently go on down the shore side by side; as we walk, and later when I leave the scene, my heart fills with respose, calmness, and peace and yes, sometimes an answer too.

June 1976. I walk where Jesus walked and so will all others until the end of time. Jesus walks with me...walks with the small Arab child, the old Jewish man transported from his native land... with the man who is crippled, alone, no one caring for him. Can I really see Jesus here or there? What must I do to open my heart's eyes, see, and feel the aloneness...narrow acceptance? So much taken for granted! Just come and go...come thousands of miles to visit...stare at...share...become. What does it matter what soil, which path, even which lake? Jesus walked...talked...healed...is everywhere...in me.

Up this steep narrow path, yes, the one made by the goats and sheep as they go to pasture. Why does He walk here? To share with me...to visit with each person who has need of Him. No village is too small, nor too isolated...He came to be Saviour...healer to all...He is today. Nothing is too unimportant to take to Him. Today I would add that I know more deeply how much He wants me to take everything to Him for healing, for sharing, for His love.

As our late evening flight took us to Holland, Eileen and I finally spoke our truth, sharing how deeply frightened we were when first in the Old City and on several other occasions. Teen-aged soldiers, each carrying a gun, were everywhere. We were more than a bit anxious, as we were obviously tourists who didn't know where we were going. We hoped that without so many soldiers about we would feel less anxious as we continued our journey.

Our car was not ready, so we walked a few blocks to the flower market for which Holland is famous. The whole street was filled with enormous displays of multicoloured tulips, and flowers of every variety and hue and perfume filled the air; a spectacular sight, several blocks long.

We did a bit of sightseeing in Amsterdam, then out into the countryside staying overnight in a small hotel in Lyden, right near an enormous windmill, which I photographed early in the morning before cars were about. The next day we traveled through northern France with its large wheat fields, many small villages, and farms. We began to note that farms seemed to have very large houses and on closer inspection found that the barns and houses were one unit. I'm not sure I would want to live that close to the barn; our own at the ranch was a long way away and still a bit stinky when the wind was right.

Our map showed that the most direct route to Chartres required going right through Paris. The traffic was horrible as it was about 5:00 PM but I kept going and suddenly saw a sign directing us to Compeigne. We turned up the ramp to ground level, drove a bit further, and stopped at a small shop to get bread, cheese, beer, and fruit for supper. Suddenly we saw the Chartres Cathedral in the distance. I pulled off to a side road, and we ate our supper. This magnificent cathedral seems to rise directly from the grassy plain, a breathtaking sight that is in view for many miles before you arrive. We stayed overnight, went to Mass the next morning and it was here that I saw my first labyrinth, for one is installed on the floor of the cathedral. We used this model to make our outdoor labyrinth at Bethlehem Retreat Centre many years later.

We stayed at a Bed and Breakfast and spent at least twelve to fourteen hours touring each day. We didn't want to miss anything, so we drove along back roads, stopping to get fruits, vegetables, cheese, and cold meats. If we ate a restaurant meal, it usually was lunch, which was far cheaper than dinner. The small villages looked like they had been unchanged for hundreds of years. The simple houses, similar in material and colour, often partially covered by vines, created a harmony that has been present for centuries. Occasionally a church steeple would show signs of repair, as would some buildings, indicating shelling, no doubt from the World Wars.

We arrived at Lourdes during the lunch hour and we were able to walk the Stations of the Cross without crowds. The bronze life-sized figures placed in natural settings on a hill up from the grotto were prayerful and I was able to take excellent pictures. We then got in the line to take a bath. It was quite an unusual spiritual experience to strip down and bathe in these cold waters as we prayed for healing. In and out of the water, shake yourself dry and re-dress. In the twilight procession, thousands of pilgrims went down to the grotto, all singing the Lourdes Hymn, *Ave, Ave, Ave Maria*. This prayerful pilgrimage with so many sick people and their volunteer caregivers made a deep impact on me. Fortunately we had found a small hotel on the outskirts and avoided the stalls selling beads and statues to tourists.

The next morning we drove through many tiny villages and farmlands, then on to the walled city of Carcassonne, and gradually made our way down the Riviera to Rome, where we were to stay at a convent. I had a good map, but we went round and round searching for street signs, and got lots of loud horn blasts sent our way. I just gave up, stopped a taxi and paid him to get us to the correct address. What a surprise. We had passed the street several times, but the sign, knocked down, lay hidden on the gravel walkway. Since this initial trip, I have driven in the British Isles and much of Europe but never have been in such chaotic traffic as that of Rome. I learned my lesson and parked my car whenever in Rome, and took public transportation, for no one obeys traffic signs, not even policemen.

Next day we met Abbot Peter Eberle who took us to a Papal audience with Pope Paul VI, held in the hall built for this purpose and seating twelve thousand; we listened to a choir until it was time for the Pope to arrive. As he was carried in by four Swiss Guards, the standing audience called out greetings in many languages, all thrilled to see and honour Paul VI as Pope. He spoke in several languages and blessed particular groups as well as the whole audience. The next day Mass was at the main altar in St. Peter's, with the Sistine Choir, many Cardinals, Bishops, and diplomats in attendance. The liturgical splendour spoke to me deeply. Church history seeped into our beings as we visited the Vatican Museum, the Sistine Chapel and ancient churches. At St. John Lateran, one kneels going up the twenty-eight marble steps, said to come from the palace of Pontius Pilate in Jerusalem. The legend is that Jesus walked these steps to and from his conviction. St. Helena brought them from Jerusalem. This kneeling walk was an incredibly difficult task because my arthritis was already limiting me; I chose to ignore the pain, as I wanted to participate in this special part of a Roman pilgrimage.

We left Rome and drove through the beautiful countryside to Assisi where we visited the Basilica, attending Mass at the tomb of St. Francis. In St. Clare's Church we prayed before the San Damiano Cross and then visited the Porziuncola chapel in the Basilica downtown. Our next stop was at Subiacco, where we walked up a long, tree-shaded path to the site of St. Benedict's cave. A monk from Australia spent a couple of hours with us and let me take pictures galore. It was a fantastic experience to be able to spend so much time enjoying the many beautiful frescoes depicting scenes from Benedict's life. We identified most of them and I was able to use my tripod and take timed shots with excellent results.

Florence and Ravenna each had so much art and history, we could have stayed a month, but it was on to Venice and over the Brenner Pass to Austria. Immediately we noticed many small, hand-painted wayside shrines, each with fresh flowers in a vase. We stopped at several to see the details that spoke of the love and care taken both in construction and in decoration. Unfortunately, we could not read German. On then to Switzerland and to the Matterhorn, where we walked in meadows, took pictures, and best of all, lay down and rolled down the hills as if we were small children. It was a real thrill to be that free and so close to the earth. It reminded me of the times I rolled down the contours at the ranch as a small child.

The next day we arrived at Engelberg, the more than thousand-year-old Benedictine Abbey that founded Mt. Angel Abbey in Oregon. We were expected, and shown to our quarters and after some visiting were served a light supper in the guest refectory—bologna sandwiches and tea with red wine. The next morning we attended Office and Mass with the monks at the Abbey church, then took the train to the monastery of Maria Rickenbach. The rail station was just a small platform and a gondola of fair size took us up to the monastery, as there is no road for autos even today. For over a hundred years all the building materials and anything needed has gone up in the gondola or up the trail on the backs of donkeys. The first things I noticed were the immaculately laid out vegetable and flower gardens and the awe-inspiring view from the top out over the other peaks of the alpine mountains. The Sisters, all still in full habits, were most gracious and showed us their monastery, explaining that they made their living by running a guesthouse as well as a small school. They had had no new members for over twenty-five years, but had a lot of faith in the future as they had just completed a new Novitiate. It was a fantastic visit and over the years, I have returned several times; the last time our entire group had Mass and lunch at the monastery. Their faith paid off; there were three new members on my last visit.

Visiting our founding monastery topped all the historic Benedictine sites we explored on our journey. Seeing the Peace sign over the door of Monte Casino, the frescos of Benedict's cave at Subiacco and now this site brought our entire heritage as Benedictines together. I certainly felt close to all the thousands of others who have called a Benedictine monastery home these past fifteen hundred years.

We went to Mannheim in Southern Germany because I remember Hank speaking of his stay there for a week or more during the winter of 1944. We attended Mass the next day, finding that the sermon was in German and the Mass itself in French. Obviously this parish, in the Alsace, served both communities and later we found they varied all their services week by week.

Then we drove on to the village of Tanville and as we entered the town, wondered how to find the Ernst family homes so we could visit the families of Sisters Colette and Odelia. We stopped to ask a young woman slowly walking on the sidewalk. We said the word "Ernst" and she immediately got excited and in her broken English asked if we were "the Sisters". A warm welcome as she called over her shoulder to others. Hugs all around.

The Sisters had asked us to see some of their family and friends and provided a list of about a dozen people. The niece of our Sisters became our guide as we visited and took pictures of each family and house to show the Sisters on our return. The sense of stability in the small village was evident as we went to the graveyard. We saw the graves marked by name and date and then one with just the Ernst family name. Every thirty or so years they open the graves, gather the bones, and put them into a family plot; the gravesite is then used for another person.

The niece asked us to stay overnight and we found this experience a real treat. Looking out the window early in the morning we saw the father of the family with a rick, a large basket on his back, going out to cut greens for his rabbits. This family had lived in this simple village for hundreds of years. The house in which we stayed was typical, I am sure, several hundred years old but showing signs of renovation to the kitchen and a very modern bathroom. The bedroom was simply furnished. No doubt, it was one of the best houses in the village.

We continued travelling toward Paris. I had not expected so many wonders around each corner. On a back road, one day, I turned the corner and there was a huge field of wheat and a farmer was using his large draft horse to pull his thresher blade through the wheat. The field was like one in the Bible when Jesus told his disciples not to pull out the weeds but let them grow until harvest time and then separate the wheat from the weeds. In this instance the weeds were red poppies, thickly spread throughout the field. I stopped the car at the edge of the road and Eileen went and sat among the poppies. Of course, it made a great picture.

After spending some time in the countryside and a short cruise on the Rhine we drove to Brussels, turned in the car and went by train to Paris. One of Sister Colette's nieces had arranged for us to have dinner at their restaurant in Paris. A couple who spoke English had noticed we had no menu and were getting special dishes. For example, the waitress brought a live fish for Eileen to approve before they cooked it. We had *patê de fois gras* and other appetizers as well as several wines. The couple was worried that our bill would be astronomical, as it was a very expensive restaurant; they were relieved to hear we were personal guests.

The largest cathedrals in Paris are mind-boggling in size and décor. As all tourists do, we strolled along the

Seine and the oldest parts of the city and included a short museum visit to see the Mona Lisa. A huge city, reeking of exhaust from modern cars, yet one gets the sense of history around every corner. Our time was excessively short to take in much but certainly, we did get the flavour of Paris and wanted to return some day.

The boat-train took us to Dover where, next morning, we picked up a car. Driving on the wrong side of the road was no simple task and Eileen screamed at me whenever I hit a curb. Gradually I managed, and we stopped at many spots we had hoped to see, from Canterbury Cathedral up to Inverness in Scotland and then back down through Edinburgh to Holy Island, visiting many of the historic Benedictine sites on the way. In London, we turned the car in and explored the city by bus or train.

We always stopped at world famous religious shrines and attended Mass at sites like Mont San Michael, Chartres, Lourdes, Sacred Heart, Notre Dame, Canterbury, Ely, York. We also tried to attend daily Mass in small village churches in all countries we visited which often showed us how other cultures lived out their Catholic faith. Changes mandated by Vatican II were still being processed as some services were in Latin, others in the native tongue of the country. It was obvious that congregations were mostly visitors in the larger shrines and cathedrals, with chatting, and a real lack of reverence. Used to daily Mass at home we stopped in small villages where we found only a few women in attendance, the Mass nearly always in Latin, no changes evident from Vatican II, with few altars facing the people.

All my life I had looked forward to visiting Europe; it was a fabulous experience and we came home happy, satiated with all the sights we had seen, the encounters on the way and great pictures. The longing "to see", which had started when I was a child listening to world travelers, was satisfied, at least for a time.

Traveling with just one companion allowed the unexpected and unanticipated to happen and so, often, it did. We set our own agenda, stopping to take pictures, and to talk, often in sign language, with the people. My photography really came into its own because there was so much of interest everywhere I turned and I had time at my disposal to get the best pictures.

Years later I enjoyed using my own positive experiences and familiarity with these countries to set up pilgrimages for groups of about thirty. In this way, the schedule was suited to the interests of our group, and we stayed away from the tourist traps. Our trip was just the first of many trips: to the Holy Lands, Europe, two pilgrimages to Turkey and Greece, a tour of the important Celtic sites in England and Ireland, and one of the special Benedictine historical sites in Europe. Eileen and I also took a month-long visit to England, Scotland, and Wales to visit some of the 125 sites that were once, or still are monasteries living according to the Benedictine Rule. I spent many months researching and documenting these sites and it was tremendous fun to finally visit and photograph 102 of them.

✠

In our Benedictine community a Junior sister may request final vows at any time between three and nine years. She usually discerns this with her director, other formation personnel, and the Prioress. Early in 1974 they felt I was ready and my request went before the community. Antoinette and Eileen came from the meeting to tell me the community had rejected my request. I was angry, upset, and deep-down bewildered. Neither Antoinette nor Eileen had anticipated a rejection.

This was a hard collision with reality. Nothing I could do could change the vote. I felt rejected through and through. Eileen and Father Henry both helped me to see that people were afraid to take a chance with me; didn't really know me. I was different, my whole life until the age of fifty was different from their own experiences. I was always busy and not living the mainstream community life, since we were living at Shalom and many of our duties were there. To some I apparently stuck out like a sore thumb and might never fit in, and they were afraid of my being so atypical.

A misfit a second time in my life. Never did I feel that I shouldn't try to live out my call. The day I was turned down I spoke to the community, at their request, and asked to have Sister Gemma appointed as my director since some of the Sisters felt Sister Eileen and I were too close as friends. I did enjoy being under Sister Gemma, a former Prioress, and college professor; we got along well. Six months later the community voted again, approving me to make final vows. Looking back on the wait for final vows, twenty-five years later, I realize I weathered the storm, supported by God's continuous call to religious life. At the time it was a near disaster but in just a few days I knew that I heard no other call. My mother and Aunt Hilda came from California for the ceremony. Because my family contingent was small, this left room for guests who had never been to a vow ceremony and several local families came with their children. We posted a general invitation to those who came to Shalom.

The making of final vows is a life-long commitment acknowledging that I belong to and will live out my life as a Benedictine of Queen of Angels Monastery; a significant milestone in my life. I felt called; I knew more testing, and more challenges to personal growth would likely be before me. I felt that the support and prayer of my community sisters would sustain me at such times of trial.

May 2001. Maybe I always had to become a Benedictine. As I read the Rule of Benedict the first word was "Listen", and in that was a call for me to read more. Likewise as a small child I was afraid of "forever and ever"; I was also hearing a call. It was such a strange insight for a small child, of this I am aware, but also that "forever and ever", not understood, was ever before my mind's eye and has been a drawing and a path for my life. Who was this God who scared me so much? It has taken nearly eighty years to begin to figure

242

out, not that there is an answer, but to understand that not only is there no answer but that is how it should be.

My Gethsemane

The trial came far sooner than I could have anticipated. In mid-December 1981, after several years of working at Shalom, the Prioress called Eileen and me to her office one afternoon. She removed me from Directorship at Shalom effective immediately. When I asked the reason, she said she would not tell me or anyone else the reason. You can imagine the shock of such an event. Condemned! The Prioress removed me from my position without telling me the charge, the person making it, or any reason for the sudden dismissal. She said that she would speak to those who came to Shalom groups and a note went up on the bulletin board informing the community.

I can't begin to tell you the shock of such an unjust decision. Unbeknownst to me Sister Eileen went back to see the Prioress the next day and spoke of the injustice of such handling of the event but she would not

244

discuss it with her. I couldn't think of anything that should have brought about such a decision. Charged, found guilty and punished. I had absolutely no knowledge of what I had done and no chance to confront evidence against me. What happened to innocent until proven guilty? Apparently two sets of justice, one for all people and another for religious. Experiencing this unreasonable treatment in a religious house just didn't seem possible.

Somehow, I survived. A few days later the Prioress asked if I would stay on for about three months until Sister Antoinette could come and take over. Sister Antoinette was in Texas running a House of Prayer but needed some turn-around time. I refused, as long as I did not know why I was guilty and didn't even know the charge. It made no sense to me that I was so bad one day I had to leave, and then a few days later was asked to stay on as a transition person. My spiritual director (priest) worked with me about this decision and my attitude toward the injustice. Strangely enough, while I was very angry at the system and the treatment I had received, I did not think of leaving the community. When my head got on straight I knew it was an unwarranted punishment, I could not understand it with my head and in no way did I hear God telling me that I should go. The Prioress had not asked me to leave the community, nor had anyone else, so I didn't. Those who came to Shalom for workshops or retreats, and some community Sisters, could not understand the situation any better than I. Obedience required me to accept it or leave.

I might add that that was twenty-four or so years ago and I now know that my decision to stay was in response to a call from God. Over these many years I have continued to do Spiritual Direction with the laity and religious, both male and female. From other Sisters I have heard similar stories, or at least, stories of judgments made without any better communication or justice than in my case. The injustice and pain certainly has had an effect on my relationships with other Sisters who knew there was something wrong, but I did not talk about it, it was pointless; gradually the event took its rightful place in my life.

March 5, 2001. I hesitated before taking a deep look at the Shalom story. Overall I know I did well with it but there are some other aspects that I need to bring out into the open, acknowledge, and heal and then allow the insights to come to my center.

The encounter came with my call to the Prioress's office where she removed me as Director of Shalom; she gave no reasons and she allowed no questions. I was shocked to say the least! I now know that a steel jacket came over me. I knew that her answer was final and that she wanted me out of there. I obeyed. Steel and all, I went on! I did not speak of any of the feelings or the unjustness or the shame or any of the tremendous pain that came, because I didn't know what to do and felt I could not say anything about the order given to me under obedience. I know I felt that I couldn't be disobedient, and was not.

I now realize the result was two-fold: One, the shell and mask that went up with Sisters and particularly with the people at Shalom; the other, no opportunity of knowing what I had done. I guess all I can say is that I survived. It was as if it was Mother all over again, shaming me, and I was mightily ashamed. In some sense, my response to all the years of Mother's abuse helped me to stand there with this life's death. This was an enormous disgrace in my life, but it was not destructive of the path on which God called me, though as I look back, it certainly could have been. I had learned early on how to survive, and survive I did. God's help here was sustaining, as was that of Eileen and Father Henry, who couldn't understand it at all. While not discussed, I know many of the Sisters prayed for me, Peppy especially.

At the time of the next election for Prioress I was eligible to vote and did not vote for the incumbent for Prioress. When we individually went forward to greet her I acknowledged her role as leader, placed my hands in hers, and wished her well. I am sure she acted as she thought best, and I had to acknowledge it if I was to go on with my religious life.

December 2005. I was in Mt. Angel last month and it was a good visit. All the Sisters always greet me lovingly. As usual I went in the evening to play cards. I was having some trouble with my heart so just stayed at the monastery, except for lunch one day with Salem friends. Looking back on the journal entry above, made over five years ago, change and growth still take place. While I live in Canada, I visit the Mt. Angel community frequently. I realize that even today I have not spoken of this event to any of the sisters in Mt. Angel, though of course nearly all of them know of it. It was obvious to all that something bad had gone on and that it was a shock to me and Eileen. Sometimes I wonder what others remember of the events affecting me and Shalom nearly a quarter century ago. No one has ever asked direct questions of me; my short statement was just accepted. Perhaps living the life has given me more compassion for others who come up against some of the stuck places in religious life. Our life certainly is not without struggle, always with us in one form or another.

My continuing on in religious life was the correct discernment; years of satisfying ministry in retreat direction has verified my decision. I enjoy the give and take of our small community here in Nanaimo and want to live out my days here. I know from my own life experience that living in a marriage with a family has its set of difficulties and often they are no more justly handled than my experience in religious life. It is in the living out of the life, day by day, in marriage or in religious life, and striving to grow as we handle the joys and disappointments encountered, that we become aware of God's presence with us in each situation. Blessing.

BELONGING

I've called you for myself
given you life... spirit... soul
you are just as I made you

I know all your story
nothing surprises Me
I love you as you are

I know each struggle...
each wondering and wandering
My love supports...
gives you great strength   life force
use it wisely and well

You are so loved
your energy, your love for others sustains you
you are strong, never alone
you have
My strength as you need

Jill, do not be afraid to go on
whatever comes you can handle
you have creative ways
embrace the future

You can do all I call you to
With my everlasting love
You can say yes

✠

A few days later, after my abrupt removal from Shalom,
I asked to go away for a time and left for Israel in January. I again stayed with the White Sisters in Bethlehem
and had a car so was easily able to explore the whole
land. I let picture taking and journaling gradually heal
the pain of this unjustifiable decision. I prayed and re-
flected, not only at religious sites in Israel and Palestine,
but also way out in the country. Still a country girl, I
loved to roam the narrow back roads between the Arab
villages and always felt safe doing so.

The Arab fields and vineyards between Bethlehem
and Hebron always attracted me. The people live in
nearby villages and daily ride out from their homes
with donkeys carrying tools, water, and food. A donkey
or horse draws a simple, single plough blade to turn the
soil. Individual holdings are often on hilly ground, only
an acre or two, so a tractor is not financially feasible.
Women still use a hand scythe to cut the wheat, then
bind it into sheaves and lay them on the ground to
dry, just as they did at the time of Christ. Many of the
women in this area still wear long black dresses with a
hand embroidered area, in red, about ten inches square
on their chest, and a white scarf on their heads.

Many parables and metaphors in scripture speak
of lamb and sheep, so common, yet so valuable to an

agrarian culture. Shepherding has changed very little since the time of Christ, mostly you see small family flocks cared for by men or young teenage boys or girls. Some sheep are brown and white, some the typical greyish white with dye on the fat tail to mark ownership. The shepherd leads his flock; the sheep walk in single file and one can sometimes hear him call one of them by name. He takes them out to pasture each day, or perhaps stays overnight in one of the many caves in the area. The sheep provide milk for cheese, wool for tents or clothing, and meat and are easy to raise on poor soil.

I had met an Arab merchant, a friend of the White Sisters, on my first trip to Israel so I dropped in to see him at his shop. He invited me to his summer home in Shepherd's Field, just on the outskirts of Bethlehem. We stopped at a fairly large plot of ground with a small cabin, slightly elevated from the ground so it could function as a sheepfold. We had a delicious romaine salad, fried baby zucchini, pita bread baked on coals and roasted lamb pieces. Super good! George's family, Roman Catholic, has lived in Bethlehem for over a thousand years. A wood carver by trade, George ran a garage and blacksmith shop and owned rental buildings. They have a large modern home in Bethlehem and I was their guest on several occasions and also a guest of George's sister and his parents, enjoying their hospitality each time I returned to the Holy Land.

Cooking and baking facilities are primitive in Old City houses and small villages. Early in the morning you can see a woman taking her bread to the community oven, balancing it in a basket on her head, supporting the basket with one hand, a toddler grabbing onto her other hand and maybe one or two small children walking along beside her. Families are large and there are no day care centres, so the mother takes the children with her when she goes to the market.

Bethphage, the village where the Palm Sunday walk originates, has a small church but I always found it locked. As I returned from checking the door I saw I had a flat tire. I gathered my tools, and started to change the tire. Along came a man, about fifty, walking with a rudimentary peg leg. He insisted he would change the tire for me. I pointed to the church and used my hands to show I tried to pull the door open. He reached in his pocket and produced the keys; he was the caretaker. In I went to view the interior, simply but artistically decorated with monochromatic friezes along all the walls, depicting the Palm Sunday walk. I thanked him for the tire change, gave him money and cigarettes, which were always well received. On return visits to Israel this site was on our list and the caretaker remembered me as the Oregon lady.

The so-called Good Samaritan Inn is a square building on the deserted road between Jerusalem and Jericho. It is typical of inns of earlier days in that there is a walled courtyard for the animals, a well, and a covered, simple shelter where a traveler could throw down his blanket. One day a friend and I left the paved road in this area and drove down the steep canyon on goat paths to the Wadi Kilt. We found water flowing there, and some wild flowers, so parked our car and went to take pictures. A bus-load of teenagers came down, got out, and jumped into the water. Suddenly we heard yelling; a man came to say a girl had a serious cut on her thigh and asked us to take them to the hospital. We packed our gear, got them into the car, and at top speed took off for Jerusalem some fifteen miles away. I tried to spot a police officer, or have one spot me, but had no luck. The hospital was clear across Jerusalem so an escort would have been helpful. We arrived at the hospital emergency to find it under security guard; the man spoke to them and they opened the barrier. While they got the girl out I sought a bathroom, so ran into the hospital. I returned to find another flat tire. The men could not make the jack work. Loud orders from a guard, speaking through a microphone from the balcony above, and others gesturing with guns, told the men changing the tire to hurry! The tire was changed and we got out of there. Not the best way to treat a Good Samaritan, but fortunately I never got in such a jam again.

My room at the convent in Bethlehem was simple, with a chest of drawers, a wood chair and a bed with a metal frame and uncovered springs; a duplicate of my room in the hostel in Prince George. One cold wet afternoon, while I was in my room reading, I lay down on the bed fully dressed. A few minutes later I got up, picked up something and then, as I sat down on the bed, the lights went out. The Sister came and fixed the fuse, one of the totally ancient ones, just outside my door. This happened three times. Sister's French and my English didn't help clarify the situation. Finally Sister came in, inspected my bed, and found that a wire had gotten under the leg of the bed and whenever I moved it shorted. It was 220 volts; I might have met my Maker right there in Bethlehem, but my rubber-soled shoes saved me.

During these months I had no structure to follow. Several hours were set aside for prayer each day. Early to Mass, usually at the Basilica in Bethlehem or at one of the churches I intended to visit that day. Lunch break often found me sitting in the car, parked at the edge of the Garden of Gethsemane, and looking over the old city as I ate. The garden was a special place for prayer and often a shepherd had a few sheep he let in to eat the new grass; a very pastoral scene, yet within the city.

One cannot walk the ground, visit the sites of the Bible stories, or observe the unchanging vistas without feeling the presence of Jesus and all those people who lived during his life on earth. His footprints are still there, inviting the visitor to walk in them; and walk I did. The Old City is so small that I often made several visits a day, walking along the Via Doloroso, stopping often in one of the tiny chapels for prayer. I did not have any fear wandering about the Old City during the daytime hours. I always had my camera gear in a backpack along with water and a snack.

The Old City has hundreds of Arab shops where you can find anything imaginable. You might find a fruit stand, then a yardage store, then the meat market or a shop with candles. All these stores are tiny, about twelve feet wide along the narrow street, and a few feet deep. Men usually run the shops and if you show any interest in making a purchase they declare all the good points of their product and will bargain with you for a time before agreeing on a price. In the Israeli section of Jeru-

254

salem, most people live in apartments. Land is scarce, money too. People shop daily in vegetable markets and other shops, and often small markets sell just one item, like spices or grains or meat. A far cry from the typical small towns of our country. Moderate-sized supermarkets, even in Jerusalem and Tel Aviv, are scarce.

There was constant conflict between the Arabs and the Jews with some serious outbreaks that caused the Old City and Bethlehem Arabs to be on strike for several days. In Bethlehem there was even rock throwing on the street, but as I drove a car with a tourist license plate I felt quite safe.

I spent a few days at the White Sisters convent in Nazareth. One of the English-speaking Sisters worked with the priests in some of the small villages, and she took me to a small convent in one village where we had lunch and visited. This village had made copper handcrafts for hundreds of years. We also went to small villages up on Mt. Hermon and to several along the Lebanon border. I personally encountered the war one day when I had stopped at a Taggert Fort to take pictures of flowers and a shot rang out just over my head. Obviously it came from Lebanon. I was terribly frightened and, seeking the safety of the car, stumbled, turning my knee severely, causing pain for several weeks. I got us out to safety but one scare was enough; after that I stayed nearer inhabited areas and away from the Lebanese border.

Over the months my head and my heart gradually let go of the unjust removal from Shalom, letting me absorb the peace found in the land of Jesus, even in the midst of chronic Arab-Israeli wars. It was a time of reclaiming my call to the Lord's service.

March 2003. Going to Israel was a good decision. God is so good. Getting in touch with the land took me back to my childhood at the ranch, and I found myself doing some of the same kind of wandering and investigating of anything that came into view. There are many narrow winding roads through the hills of Israel and hardly ever did I encounter a car. I was able to walk well at the time, and spent hours hiking over some of the land near the site of the battle between David and Goliath and around Ein Karem and the two Emmaus sites. Flowers were everywhere, tiny, due to the poor soil, but rich colours of red, blue, and yellow as well as white. Some roads were no more than goat paths, but driving slowly helped me find different flowers, especially the wild cyclamen, the national flower. Orchids grow at the edge of the woods often hiding among the old leaves. On Mt. Tabor I crawled through a fence into a meadow with several steers, and found orchids of various colours, with many small flowers on each foot-high stem. Hiking was a wonderful way to unwind and I left some of my pressures and tensions there in the woods. I experienced many healing "Aha" moments and had many good talks with God, mostly without words, just absorbing His/Her Presence from all about me. I was ready to return to Mt. Angel, sure that I was being called to continue life as a Benedictine.

WHOLENESS

Become whole not new or old ...
God called   formed   shaped
yet
I sense an incompleteness
this hunger for God
stirs me   beckons
I long for God with gnawing empty sensations

Hungry
I become broken shattered   rough edged
I must die

Growth is painful
dark to light pain in all new creation
in weakness,
searching exploring experiencing my humanness

In wholeness no part of me is unacceptable, unloved
risk   opening
vulnerable

Finding myself
leads to centeredness
am nourished deep within
my heart touches God

Centered, balanced with God's peace
am not blown by wind
thrown by struggles
or drowned by sorrow

Aware of my humanity   gifts
my outreach is to life
so, God, draw me
I will follow

When I returned from Israel I continued to see people
for spiritual direction and gave individual and group
retreats as well as continuing with my work in Lake
Oswego. I had already been involved in writing the series *Priory Productions* that were filmstrips with music
and meditation. They were rather popular with some
of the retreat houses and with hospitals that used them
as part of their spiritual offering for short meditations
on their in-room televisions. It was surprising to me
how well they sold. In addition, I wrote a book, *Foundations Last Forever*, that discussed Lectio Divina as a
prayer form. I did significant research for it and really
felt my own Lectio improved markedly as a result. This
small book's illustrations were pictures taken in old abbeys and monasteries in England and Scotland. The
scripture/question book, *Seek Abide*, has also sold well.
Individuals have used *His Way My Way*, as have various
study groups who wanted to do this type of in-depth
growth journaling. I continued to give retreats, either
at Shalom or at specific parish centres or for other de-
nominations. My work with individuals continued as
before, using office space in Howard Hall at the mon-

astery. Sister Eileen accompanied me on most of these retreats and prayed for individuals as requested. My ministry was fulfilling and I was enjoying living at the monastery.

JOURNEY'S END, JOURNEY'S BEGINNING

Bishop Remi De Roo of the Diocese of Vancouver Island, B.C., sought a Benedictine Community presence on the Island and took his request to the Federation of St. Gertrude meeting in Oregon. Sisters from Queen of Angels Monastery had served at Kakawis, a school for native children on Meares Island, B.C., from 1900 to 1960. The Sisters, he said, could choose their own location as well as area of ministry. Sister Augusta Marie Raabe OSB and Sister Jean Ann Berning OSB discerned individually, and then shared their interest in going to Vancouver Island to establish that presence. They first asked permission to start a foundation in 1972, but not until mid-summer of 1974 did the community grant it.

The Sisters made several trips to the Island and chose Nanaimo as the site of their new monastery. They were to minister, at least in part, through St. Peter's parish, and would live in Rockridge, a house owned by the parish. On their previous trips to Nanaimo they had met a number of people who were willing to support them as they set up their home and ministry. Sisters Augusta, Jean Ann and Anne Ryan, who had decided to join with them, arrived in Nanaimo on September 10, 1972.

About a year later they bought property at 2940 Killarney St. for their monastery and a few years later they purchased the house next door. Sisters Judith Hennigan and Roberta Dyer joined them for a period of time and then returned to Mt. Angel, as did Anne Ryan. Sister Augusta taught scripture classes and did spiritual direction; Jean Ann did parish work, then took her degree in counselling and worked at the Nanaimo Regional General Hospital. Sister Claudia May had felt called to join the Sisters; she was caring for her aged parents and was only able to come in 1981. She immediately started taking care of two children while their parents worked.

In the fall of 1982 Sister Augusta died, leaving only Sisters Jean Ann and Claudia to continue with ministry. The Prioress told Sisters Claudia and Jean Ann that if they didn't get another sister within a year they would have to sell one of their two houses. I remember hearing that announcement and remarked to my mother and sister, who were visiting me, that if I had any courage I would offer to go for a year. Selling one of the houses the Sisters and their local supporters had worked so hard to obtain just made no sense to me, as they would lose money and markedly restrict their ministry. My call to Canada had begun, though I did not know it then.

The next summer I offered to give a weekend retreat in Nanaimo in September, without charge. Sister Jean Ann did a good job of selling the need for another Sister, as many of the group spoke to me of this need and some openly invited me to come live at the House of Bread. The evening after the retreat Jean Ann took her Hibachi, sausages and other fixings and we had a barbeque picnic at Piper's Lagoon. This Lagoon looks out across several small islands to Vancouver and is a spot to watch the ferries and sailboats pass on their way to Nanaimo. Jean Ann, Eileen and I talked a long time about the ministry in Nanaimo and I carried some of this conversation with me into the night. It was nearly a year since Augusta's death and no other Sisters had offered to move to Nanaimo.

As I sat at breakfast the next morning I was overwhelmed with the knowledge that I had to offer to serve in Nanaimo; do it right then. I asked to speak to Jean Ann and told her that if they wanted me to do so, I would ask to come for a year to help their ministry. She talked with Claudia and they decided right then that they would take a chance with me. I know that both Sisters Antoinette and Eileen, who were with me on that trip, were shocked when they heard of my offer to go to Nanaimo. On arriving home I met with Sister Alberta, received permission to go to Canada for a year, and left in just a couple of weeks; I planned to do the retreats already booked by driving down from Canada.

I lived in 2940 Killarney and Claudia and Jean Ann lived next door at 2950. Since both of them worked, Claudia doing child care and Jean Ann counselling at the hospital, I cooked the dinner, which I enjoyed making. Retreatants came to stay in the house I lived in, usually on weekends, but occasionally for a longer time. We also had a study group or two. Very quickly I organized an ecumenical group in Duncan that went on for years. Another group formed in St. Elizabeth's parish in Sydney.

The community had signs of new life. Valerie Swenson, a psychiatric nurse, our first Canadian, entered and was in the process of incorporation into our community. I was busy with a gradually increasing workload, but living in such close quarters with guests did not give them the privacy they needed. It was difficult to schedule groups at the same time as private retreatants. I began to discern, and my question was, "Should I return to Mt. Angel, since my year in Nanaimo has stretched to three?"

A realtor we knew had repeatedly asked me to look at property he felt would be ideal for our community—a very large house on a local lake. The price was so high I saw no point in making any investigation even though all of us knew we needed a better arrangement for guests. The next time the realtor called, I said I would look at the property just to put an end to his calls. We drove up into the hills and parked in front of a huge building; I could just see a bit of a lake. From inside, the view was spectacular; one looked across a large lawn to the lake and the mountain in the background. The spacious, modern, three-story building had large rooms, and appropriate renovations could transform it into a great retreat center. I hid my enthusiasm from the realtor, went back, and talked it over with Jean Ann and Claudia. Jean Ann and I realized we would have to sell both properties to make the purchase and it could be too great a financial risk. We let it go. Little did I know, in early January, 1987, what the Lord had in mind for us.

The Diocese of Victoria knew of the property and, when the price kept dropping, decided to buy it if we, the Benedictines, would run it as a retreat house. That was a touchy decision; we did not know how to set up the best relationship with the Diocese, as I did not want to work for them. One of our friends, an experienced businessman, met with us and we worked out a list of twenty requirements to present to the Diocese. These included a twenty-five-year lease of the premises, with the Benedictines in charge of all programs and ministry. Renovations to the building, or construction of new buildings, would be our responsibility and our method of paying rent. The Bishop accepted our lease offer and the Diocese bought the property. When the Diocese completed the sale on February 19, 1987, Claudia and I moved in. We had two beds, a couple of lamps, a refrigerator, stove, a card table, and a couple of chairs. We found out only when we arrived that we had no heat at all. The three heat pumps were all down, but we got heat the next day. There were six fireplaces, all useless, as we didn't have any wood. Bethlehem was born.

Lay support for our ministry at Bethlehem came early, with many women and men volunteering services.

Some helped us build, others gathered furnishings and other supplies. We welcomed used furniture and appliances and made many trips to the "Sally Ann".

We were introduced to some refugees from Fiji who offered to come help us by doing work around the grounds, with our new computer, and in the office. Their status as refugees precluded employment. Warm friendships followed, and the family is still among our close friends.

July 2004. No one could have predicted the complex tale of joys and woes and years of hard work that made Bethlehem what it is today. It welcomes all religious and non-profit groups and individuals who want to come to a place of peace and quiet for refreshment and new hope. It has been a strongly ecumenical ministry all these years, giving us an opportunity to work with many individuals and a wide variety of groups. I truly feel that our community of three Sisters and a Junior Sister could not have envisioned a ministry of this scope as we undertook the founding of Bethlehem Retreat Centre. If I had known the future and all its struggles, I probably wouldn't have undertaken the ministry at all, or just maybe I would.

The only building was the large three-story house, about eight years old, quite neglected, as it had been vacant for more than a year. We did extensive renovations to each floor. We enlarged the kitchen, added an extra oven, and installed a commercial dishwasher to bring the food service up to par. The renovation work-week was Monday to Friday morning. On Friday afternoon we cleaned up the drywall, and the general mess, made the beds, and welcomed guests. Our first two guests arrived in April. The City of Nanaimo would not allow us to use some of the space in the main building for bedrooms, so quite early we built Capernaum, with eighteen rooms. Money was in short supply, so Claudia and I, both in our sixties, tried to make up for it by doing as much as possible ourselves. It was a huge undertaking, as each projected renovation always turned up unexpected snarls.

Ingenuity was the name of the game. My talent for sizing up space and making things fit came into good use. We had a serious problem with the main floor carpet, as we didn't have enough to complete the upstairs hall extension and it had to match. After a day or so of looking around I realized that the main floor powder room had enough of the matching carpet to do the job. So up it came and the hall got patched. The dining room buffet, when taken apart, became a counter in the kitchen. Changes everywhere, with work held up sometimes as we needed to find more money. As the workload increased, we added more staff for the grounds as well as within the house.

When the Bishop wanted Bethlehem to be the site for the Synod, we soon found we had to add a chapel/meeting room. He spoke to us about it in September and the first Mass was held there on Christmas Eve. The carpet wasn't in yet, but heat was on and chairs available. It has been a well-used building, housing not only our Catholic Mass on Saturday but other religious services as well, and also serving as a large meeting space.

It has excellent acoustics and some college and other music groups request it for rehearsals. In 1990, Sister Eileen had a sabbatical year and came to Nanaimo for some months. While at a House of Prayer in Oklahoma she discerned that she would come to Bethlehem for her next assignment; she was here for the next eight years, working in all aspects of the retreat ministry.

One day Sister Eileen and I were talking with a couple of retreatants and mentioned that it would be wonderful if the House of Bread Monastery could be closer to us here on the lake. That evening one of them called to say she knew a couple who had property just down the road, five acres, with a rather new house, that they were thinking of placing on the market. I talked with Jean Ann and then made contact with the couple. We were able to buy the five acres of waterfront property without a realtor. The house, though quite new, needed a number of things done to make it practical for community living; four bedrooms and two baths were added. The great moving day to 2329 Arbot Rd. took place in July, 1991.

Not only did we get a new monastery up at the lake but a number of women decided to give their call to monastic life a test. Over the years a number of women came, stayed for a few months to several years, and then left to resume their lives elsewhere. In July, 1990, Dr. Patricia Brady asked to begin the process of becoming Benedictine. She was a former Poor Clare in Duncan and in the last several years was on the staff of the Cathedral in Victoria. She has been a mainstay at Bethlehem, leading several scripture classes, conducting retreats and doing spiritual direction. Sister Rose Mary

267

Terhaar of Mt. Angel transferred to House of Bread in December 1990. Rosie has been treasurer, as well as using her creativity in making pottery and herbal products; she is a certified Herbologist. Sister Barbara Rinehart, a Holy Name sister, officially transferred and now Barb is a counsellor at the Bethlehem Counselling Centre. Sister Mary Ann Gisler, a social worker and counsellor, also came from Mt. Angel in 1992. The community has continued to grow and there are now nine in perpetual vows and a Junior Sister and two candidates.

In January, 1993, Queen of Angels Monastery approved the House of Bread to become an independent monastery of the Federation. On June 23, 1993, Sister Jean Ann Berning OSB was elected Prioress for a term of four years and was installed on July 11, the Feast of St. Benedict. This was a formal religious ceremony, with our former Prioress of Mt. Angel, Sister Dorothy Jean Beyer transferring to Sister Jean Ann the records and papers of each sister. The Federation President then presided at the ceremony of installation in which all of us took part. We had many guests for the service and reception and they spoke of how happy they were that we were now a true Canadian community. The only other English-speaking Benedictine monastery for women in Canada is in Winnipeg.

We needed more living space to meet the needs of our growing community. A second major building on the monastery property, Benedict, was completed and a blessing and open house held on the 8th of May. Sisters, in order to save money, painted the siding, kept the site clean and did other jobs that helped the builders speed up the process.

Sister Germaine Chrupalo transferred to our community from St. Benedict's in Winnipeg and worked at her nursing profession in a care facility for some years. Now retired, Germaine is into vegetable gardening, caring for the Llamas and baking. Karen Nicol of Vancouver is a Junior Sister. Sister Phyllis Mayer of Vancouver transferred, making her monastic profession in September 2004. Sadly, Phyllis died of cancer in February, 2005.

Community life requires a special gift from God, but by putting together each Sister's talents we manage to cover all the bases needed to run our own home. We have our prayer in common in the morning at Benedict House, and evening prayer in the house where we eat dinner. Our Associates also pray with us, as they are able, nearly always on weekends and most mornings. Because of a shortage of priests we do not have Mass on a daily basis. On Saturday at 4:30 we celebrate Sunday Mass at Bethlehem, with about a hundred lay people joining us. Each of us sets our own time for personal prayer and Lectio or divine reading. Our prayer schedule does not follow all the hours of the time of Benedict, and here at House of Bread we only gather together for morning and evening prayer as a community. In larger monasteries, like Mt. Angel, the Sisters who are able to do so gather for noon prayer and Compline or night prayer as well. We no longer have holy reading at meals, using the time for catching up with each other as our lives are so varied.

Sisters take turns cooking and are responsible for chores both inside and outside the houses. We have extensive vegetable gardens and they and the orchard give us much of our summer produce. Part of the diminishment of aging is that Claudia and I just can't do some things, so we are excused.

✠

My travels exploring new territories, sharing the finds and joys with others, were one way I learned to satisfy my insatiable curiosity about the world and how others lived. As I previously said, I had contact with many people from a variety of countries as a child. In 1976, the opportunity to travel to Israel and then Europe became a reality. It was but the tip of the iceberg, as repeated trips to far away lands became possible. During my visit to Israel in 1981 I investigated in depth the culture and lives of Israelis and Palestinian Arabs, and the birthplace of my Christian faith. Retreat houses often sponsor pilgrimages to Christian sites presenting a meaningful spiritual experience. Over the next several years, with the help of Sister Eileen, I organized pilgrimages to Israel. On the way home we arranged stops in Rome, Assisi and Subiacco, the cave of St. Benedict.

In 1995, we organized a trip for thirty-five of us to the major Benedictine abbeys and monasteries in southern Germany, Italy, France, and Switzerland, where we visited Engelberg, the motherhouse of Mt. Angel Abbey in Oregon, and Maria Rickenbacker, the founding monastery of Queen of Angels in Oregon.

My childhood interest in Mont San Michel and Chartres, and my visits there in 1976, made them a must for our group. The Cathedral at Vezelay, where St. Bernard preached the Second Crusade, is a former Benedictine abbey on a high hill overlooking a large valley where the Crusaders gathered to hear Bernard. There is a legend that a relic, a bone of the arm of Mary Magdalene, lies in the crypt of this church, now staffed by Franciscans. All Benedictine sites seem to be on mountain tops and it was a hard climb for me, taking a good half hour to make my way there, but worth it.

Later we went to the birth place of Scholastica and Benedict in the small Italian village of Nursia, miles off the beaten path. Our visit coincided with the Feast of Benedict, so our Benedictine chaplain concelebrated with diocesan priests, adding an unexpected blessing to our visit. We also went to Monte Cassino and Subiacco. Most of the participants were Benedictine Sisters or oblates so walking in the footsteps of our long tradition helped us sense the importance of Benedictines to Europe; St. Benedict, the founder of our order is the Patron of Europe.

Following the journeys of St. Paul we travelled to Turkey and Greece to visit the Seven Churches of the Apocalypse and the beautiful city of Istanbul, with its churches now turned into mosques. We crossed over to Asia, taking a small tourist boat across the Bosphorus, and looked back at the city, breathtaking to be sure. Our second Turkish tour started in Ankara, then took us to Cappadocia, where we found many tiny churches, from the third and fourth centuries, cut into the soft sandstone, beautifully covered with frescos of scenes from the life of Jesus. I had always wanted to visit this area, having seen pictures of the chapels in magazines as a child. It was hard for me to walk up the rather steep hillsides. Some of the able-bodied men helped by pushing me and my walker up the hills, making sure I was safe. It was one of the highlights of the entire Turkish tour and I was happy not to miss it.

Istanbul was as exciting on the second visit as on the first; fabulous setting and mosques galore. Everyone we met on these trips was friendly and helpful. In Konya we visited the museum, viewing the many dioramas depicting the living quarters and history of the whirling dervishes. That evening we arranged for a master, three musicians, and four dancers who performed their traditional spiritual dance for our group. Their faces were in a trance-like state as they danced.

We crossed over to Greece and took in the historic sites of Thessolonika, Phillipi and on down through Meteora visiting the fabulous monasteries, centuries old, built on mountain peaks. Then we made our way down to Corinth and on to Athens. Each day we had morning prayer on the bus, Mass celebrated at a special site, and readings from Acts speaking of the immediate area.

I never knew where our next excursion might take us. When we were in England we had visited Canterbury Cathedral several times. One day I noted in the paper that there was to be a large celebration of the fourteen-hundredth anniversary of the founding of Canterbury Cathedral by St. Anselm. Scheduled special services at the Cathedral, and those at nearby Benedictine Ramsgate Abbey enticed us. We invited Esther De Waal, an

English historian and biographer of Benedict, to meet us at Canterbury. Esther had lived at Canterbury for several years while her husband was Dean of the Cathedral. The history of the Cathedral and its association with St. Benedict fascinated her and she wrote *Seeking God,* which has drawn many to seek further information about Benedictines. So we organized a tour starting at Canterbury guided by Esther, until we reached Wales.

From there we gradually made our way across southern England, stopping at Glastonbury, a spiritual site for over five thousand years that includes remains of a Benedictine abbey. We also visited other Benedictine sites, Salisbury Cathedral, Tintern Abbey and St. David's in Wales, our final stop. From there we crossed the Irish Sea to visit the remains of many Celtic monasteries. We spent two nights on the Aran Islands and, after delightful sunny days exploring the history of the Celts in Ireland, we crossed over to Scotland to the Island of Iona. In the year 563, St. Columba went from Ireland to found a Celtic monastery there. In the Middle Ages it was the site of a Benedictine abbey and today is an ecumenical spiritual center. After Edinburgh, we visited Holy Island, Fountains Abbey, and York Minster, all at one time abbeys living according to the Rule of Benedict. This was again an incredible experience and gave us a chance to study and appreciate our Benedictine and pre-Benedictine monastic history in the British Isles. Roots are important in order to understand the long history of our church, particularly for those in religious life, for St. Benedict started the first order in 480 AD. Being a Benedictine and interested in history and culture, I have been blessed to have had so many on-site opportunities.

✠

By May, 1999, I had been having a great deal of difficulty with arthritis in my knees; and most often used a walker, and was well on my way to needing a wheel-chair. My pulse was far too low, in fact, on two occasions I set off the alarm at the emergency room. I went to Oregon to see my former heart specialist, who recommended a pacemaker but was aghast at the condition of my knees and said I should see a surgeon in Salem. Orthopedists here would not do surgery because of my age and the fact that both knees needed replacements. I returned to Oregon in a month and the orthopedist's first words were, "I could put in two total knee replacements, under local, in less than three hours, and you would be on your feet the next day." Well, I was surprised. I got the pacemaker in Victoria, where the cardiologist told me I should have had it years before.

The knee surgery took place in early July. I must say that I did not like to hear the Striker saw as they cut my bones off and readied them to accept the appliances, nor the pounding that was required to seat the prosthesis well. A spinal does not take away sound. Each knee has $3500 worth of some kind of metal that sounds off any wand used in airports. I was on my feet on the second day, in hospital for about four days, then went to a rehabilitation unit where I had physiotherapy four times a day. I walked well by day ten, and went back to the monastery in Mt. Angel for recovery.

I stayed at Mt. Angel for a week and a half to recover my strength and then Sister Val brought the van so I could lounge in the back seat with my legs up, which I did as we went through Vancouver. As we approached the ferry line there was a three-ferry wait. I knew it would be impossible for me; the day had already been far too long. We showed my handicapped sticker and the guard sent us on down the hill. Further along, a very young man came up and asked what we needed. I told him of the recent surgery and the need to make the first ferry possible. He asked for a letter from the doctor but we had not thought to get one. I said I could pull down my slacks and he could see the red scars of recent surgery. That got us moving and we were able to take the car on the ferry that was just about to pull out. What luck. I really doubt that I would have been able to manage on my own.

1999 held another special event for me. In mid-December I celebrated my Silver Jubilee, twenty-five years of vows. My daughter Jean and son Hal came, as did friends from Oregon and from our area of Canada. Bishop Remi De Roo celebrated the Mass and Sister Mary Ann Gisler gave the reflection. It was a celebration of my religious life and a chance to say "Thank you" to many friends who have journeyed with me. I had jokingly said as I was planning to have knee surgery that if I had a good result I would dance at my Jubilee. And so, at the end of Mass, Hal stood and told the guests of my statement and then asked, "Mother, may I have this dance?" It was the most special dance of my life, though we only danced to a few bars of "Morning Has Broken".

As the Twentieth Century came to a close Bishop De Roo gave several reflections relating to freedom, land, and future. I found this a time of deep reflection, realizing that as I made my first vows, I did not think I would live to see the turn of the century. But here I was.

January 6, 2000. Looking for peace of soul so I will know where and how to go next.

✠

Over the years the facility and our work load continued to grow and we looked forward to completing our twenty-five year lease. Our contract with the Diocese called for us to build and keep up all the buildings, so we borrowed money, built an adequate facility, and then let the increased business pay off the loans. It was working well for us. On property the Bishop purchased next door, we built and furnished Nazareth; our overnight space now had thirty rooms. Suddenly, financial problems in the Diocese placed the whole complex in jeopardy. How would it affect us?

I was returning from vacation in California, stopping for a few days at Brookings, a small city on the Oregon border, when we got the news that Bethlehem was up for sale. I never saw so many faxes sent and received. It was a huge shock, and even when I read the newspaper articles faxed to me, I could not really take it all in. In my wildest imagination I could not have predicted all the fallout that would so seriously impact our ministry at Bethlehem Retreat Center and our future.

I had been the Director of Bethlehem Retreat Center since early 1987, and our Benedictine community had spent fifteen years building up a very strong retreat ministry. Now our continuing leasehold was in doubt. I did know that there was nothing I could do by returning home more quickly than planned, so continued on the much-needed vacation, praying the meanwhile that the chaos would find resolution over time.

August 2000. It is hard to separate sorrow, loss, hurt, anger, fear, and all the other things. The future is totally unclear, but then what else is new. This has happened many times before, but with an adjustment here or there, the course straightens, or at least, is a bit clearer. It's hard not to be judgmental when reality creeps in. There could be huge fall out, a serious concern for us all. A deep question for me! Can I go on? Should I? How much can or should I stand and if I do stand, will it do any good at all? This is a crucial area, as much of the happenings are out of my magic touch. Do I have the choice about staying on here at Bethlehem? I don't feel burned out, though I am seventy-seven, just hurting for all the people who really gain by our being here and all others who come with their groups.

The House of Bread Monastery has been involved in retreat ministry here in Nanaimo for

277

more than twenty-five years and the possibility of forcing us out of existence seems neither sensible nor right. I realize my God has given me an enormous amount of strength and fortitude and those gifts are still with me, but I seem to be losing sight of them because of the urgency of this crisis. It is really not possible to divorce myself from the downfall of something that is going so well. The counsellors also suffer from this forced change, because they need this space to continue their ministry.

I cannot fathom starting something new. Way too old to ask more of myself! I feel that I cannot do it, it is just too hard and asks a "dying of self" that I am not at all aware God is asking of me. My life is nearly over, and I am responsible not to make it easier or be lazy, but also not to deliberately close it out before my time. All my life I have had a creative visioning and the urge to make it happen. Right now I want to run away and hide for a few days, but I know that is not responsible or good.

A good part of the pain comes from knowing some half-truths that one can't talk about. How to plan for the future when it really looks black; how to grey it; I don't know. What is my responsibility here? I can't go around saying, even to the community, that I don't want to go the last mile. Is God preparing me for a healing unto death and I am saying, "Not yet Lord"? Maybe I am entitled to say I can't give any more and still be me. If I am true to myself, I must go with my deepest heart feelings, those that are so painful to express. I fear rejection by some who will think and perhaps say, "Why can't you go on until the way is clear?"

I know with all undertakings I can see a vision, a future, a dream, and have had the strength, the courage, and the stamina to accomplish it, whatever it is. It is not like me to fail and I have so many strengths in spite of my weaknesses... but where and how to go on?

My deepest fears pointed out the difficult journey I had to take for the next two years before Bethlehem Retreat Centre would again gain stability. I just took care of the tasks before me, knowing that somehow the directions would come as I took a step into the unknown. Typical of my pattern. It was nearly two years before I heard the signal that I should not go forward on my personal journey alone, but needed the guidance of a Sister in Duncan.

The next two-and-a-half years were extremely stressful for all of us in our community. Not only was our retreat ministry in jeopardy but the counselling center was as well. Sister Rose Mary and I spent many a day looking for property where we could continue our ministries. There just was nothing suitable, nor could we find property to build upon within a half-hour of our monastery. A greater distance would not be practical.

Showing the facility to interested buyers was one of the hardest tasks I faced. There was a group interested in purchasing the facility, who visited us several times. They wanted to have the staff stay on so that the whole operation could continue for some months after the purchase. Their immediate intent seemed to be a mixture of a conference centre and resort. They asked me if I would work for them, even offered a high salary, but I certainly never entertained that idea.

I had already had a difficult talk or two with the business office of the Diocese regarding the sale of the property. We were facing cancellation of our lease before we had the opportunity of recovering our investment. We had put up many hundred thousands of dollars that we would have recovered as we completed the years of our lease. Sudden cancellation of the lease would require a cash settlement to cover this money we had already advanced. I went to see the Bishop about the cancellation and presented our demand for $500,000 to cover the eleven years still to run on our lease. It was some meeting. I can tell you that this was the hardest business deal of my life. When the Bishop saw me to the door he said that justice would be done. I shook so hard it took nearly the whole drive home before any kind of normal feeling returned to my body. It even took time to gather my forces and reply to the questions of Mary Ann and Rose Mary.

February 28, 2001. One of God's gifts to me has been to be there for other people and throughout the years I have often been the strong one. I have managed some hard times in my family and out of it. I remember that Dad called me when Jack died and wanted me to be there with him to make the arrangements. Even Mother depended on me on several occasions when she was seriously ill and I did what I could, and probably rather graciously.

I have been there for countless others and tried to give as needed. But I have not allowed myself to let others really do for me. There have been a few people, but not many. Trust issues and shame make it difficult to express my real needs.

I realize that now I need to become congruent if I am going to continue to do what will be before me these next months. Sometimes my strength and vision are a real block to an equal give and take. I need to try to evaluate major movements and directions in the light of what is my responsibility and how much I can safely give to it. I do not need to do it all; there are some things I just need to stop doing, or stop sooner, so that I am not worn out but still of use. This goes right back to listening to my body. There have been many things that have been hard for me this year, particularly physical challenges, and I must pay attention to them. I must also pay attention to the special body changes that aging has brought forth. Someone sixty-five or so really doesn't realize the inevitable physical losses that will come later; fifteen years make a huge difference.

I seem sometimes to look at what I can't do, rather than what I still can do. I must take time to sort this out and then follow my truth as best I can. The negativity is just another put-down of myself...another feeling of shame because I can't do whatever is needed any longer. I realize this goes back to earliest days. But I know better now, have at least heard different ways, and have experienced some of them. Sometimes I forget that I have a right to choose how I will be and I must do this even more.

I have a heart of mechanical gadgets, or at least that is how it runs but I still have a heart of flesh which I saw beating, wires and all...and it is from that heart, helped so that it is stronger than in past years, that I can mend the brokenness of my life and continue to keep up the beat put there by God, through the hands of the doctors. It is still in the right place and I must honour the feelings that come as my heart is touched.

FEEL LOVE

Touched, I go on
destination unsure
on the way   be with
You forever more

Life spotted
roughness apparent
challenges always there supported

Cleavage of heart obvious
divisions clarified
everlasting love melts my heart.
pain less   beat regular   nourishing

Your presence in my heart
a new way

Feel love   trust
heart cared for differently
thank you, God

On March 21, 2001, the Feast of St. Benedict, it suddenly came to me that the only way our ministry could
continue was to take a huge leap and buy the facility.
This would be a great financial risk but would allow us
to continue our work without interruption. I took the
idea to a community meeting and the Sisters agreed
that very night that we should investigate the purchase
from the Diocese. From an operational standpoint, we
would need to have both pieces of property, as Nazareth
had bedrooms and the trees on that property helped
preserve our peaceful atmosphere. We decided to offer
to purchase the initial portion of Bethlehem and lease
the second portion and would need time to do fund-
raising to make the purchase possible.

The House of Bread community has been commit-
ted to offering spiritual opportunities on the Island
since 1974. Somehow, it seemed right that the Sisters
make the sacrifices to purchase Bethlehem for the good
of the ministry. As a religious community we were not
really interested in owning the facility but, if ministry
in the Counselling Center and the Retreat work was
to continue, there was nothing else we could do. Ten
women taking on such a burden speaks of our courage
and trust in the future, for sure.

I went to the Diocesan office to present a formal offer. This was early in April and we asked for a year to

close the purchase, but they gave us only until December 1st to raise $1.8 million dollars. They would apply the $500,000 lease cancellation to the price of the first portion, thus bringing it down to $1.3 million. They agreed to lease us the Nazareth property for two years with the option to purchase it at $420,000. I was very disheartened. It looked like an insurmountable task to raise $1.3 million in just under seven months. The only thing to do was to try.

The next steps we took are now history. We hired fundraisers to advise us and started a drive, doing all the usual worrying this kind of undertaking presents to anyone. Immediately we called on our friends, those who had supported Bethlehem through the years, and they came on board, helping to support our endeavour. One of my personal jobs was to try to raise money by calling religious organizations throughout Canada and, to some extent, in the U.S.A. I also contacted some of the Benedictine monasteries to see if any could loan us some bridge financing, and was pleased that the necessary amount was forthcoming.

One of the fundraising events was a large Treasure Auction totally organized by a group of lay friends. It did not take them long to organize all the details, large and small, that went into such an endeavour. They received wonderful donations, and volunteers came forward to set up and supervise the sale. There were many couples and single people from up and down the Island, and even some from Vancouver, who worked on the day of the sale. It was a massive undertaking, but with so many helpers, it was a great success. Tables displaying auction items were placed in the chapel and in the large room in the main building, and the many treasures that they held sold well. Air Cadets took over the parking and men from the Knights of Columbus watched the doors. The auction raised over $25,000 for the purchase fund. It was a fantastic opportunity for publicity and to show Bethlehem and its facility to many who had never been there before.

In late November, 2001, we purchased the first portion of Bethlehem, consisting of the main building, chapel, and Capernaum. The fundraising continued and the second piece, the site of the Labyrinth and Nazareth, was purchased in the fall of 2002 with the help of a healthy mortgage, which is a very heavy burden on a non-profit society.

Those years presented some horrendous tasks for me, personally, as I was still running Bethlehem as a retreat facility, and was also very involved in the fundraising process. The hardest part was to become a beggar—calling people and asking for money is just not my style. I was quite successful, thanks to the generosity of people who wanted to support the retreat ministry, though they might be thousands of miles away. These were some of the hardest years of my life, and I was not young. At the time I knew I was working to the level where I was too tired every day, and it finally caught up with me, but only after we accomplished our goal and made the purchase.

February 1, 2003. The last several years have been times of too much going on. I felt the need to give up then, but the sisters asked me to stay, so I did.

I get so tired that sometimes I cringe at the thought of someone asking me to do more. If so, it is as though I am a snake tightly coiled and waiting for someone to touch me or maybe even walk a bit on my territory. The direct opposite of where I want to be. I want to feel God's love for me as I am, even as a snake in the grass. Later in the day, when sharing with my spiritual director about this, I got a shaking chill in my chest, it was as if God had just smacked me.

BRC is not God's call for me now. I need community to verify that I have done all I can and more than I ever expected was possible. They need to understand that I can no longer do it. Let joy come up and begin to enjoy old age.

I have gone against the grain, against my insights and desires, these past two years...three years, really. I have not gotten by with it. No amount of good can replace the loss. I need to accept it and move on or there will be no future for me, and that is wrong. It will be self abuse and that cannot go on any more; not my call.

When does shakiness come? When intense feelings are under the surface. I try to hold back on acknowledging them, ashamed of the content or intensity or both. Like I shake when I reveal my real self to another. Good or bad stuff doesn't matter. I guess it is mostly shame when I am not in control of my neediness and my shaking. Like an eighty year old finds it unacceptable to show what is truly there.

In March, 2003, a friend asked how I would feel if some people got together to celebrate my life. It took some talking for me to say yes, but the result has had a far-reaching effect in my life. It scared me to think of people saying what they found good, funny, or unique about me. This was a first for me, to have to sit there and let others tell me about myself. Of course I did not know who was going to share a memory and that added to my fear. Some of my own memories of the past twenty years needed to be in the closet, or deep down wherever one stuffs them. I was sure I would squirm too much or feel embarrassed, and I must say that that was true.

A general invitation went out to those who knew me here in Nanaimo. Friends also came from Oregon, Calgary, Vancouver and other parts of Vancouver Island. Each person who chose could tell a story or relate a memory that somehow touched them. There were about fifteen people who spoke. They each could speak for only eighty seconds, one for each year of my life. If they spoke too long, Dan Mulligan interrupted them by ringing a bell. Some of the memories brought out the typical Jill, yet all were different and long forgotten by me. Sister Eileen was not able to attend, but sent a letter longer than eighty seconds' worth; guess she could not hear Dan's bell down in Oregon.

As the crowd gathered they sang several of my favourite songs. At the conclusion I thanked them for coming, told them about some of the firsts in my life, and recounted some of my own memorable occasions from long before I came to Canada. I spoke about the thrill of walking across the Golden Gate Bridge on the first day and driving across the Bay Bridge on opening day. Another special memory was that I attended the opening of the World's Fair on Treasure Island, as well as its close, in 1940. On the final day, Carrie Jacobs Bond sang her own composition, "The End of a Perfect Day". I always treasured that memory and Sister Mary Ann sang that song beautifully to bring that part of the celebration to a close.

We then went to the View room for wine and cheese and I was able to greet each of the guests individually. It was a tremendously heart-opening event and touched me deeply. Sister Mary Ann announced, at the Memorable Moments in early April, that the event was not a retirement party. But within two weeks I started to suffer from heart failure and in late July the doctor insisted that I retire. I had intended to stay on through September, to make the transition a bit easier for a new Director, but was unable to do so.

BECOMING AT HOME IN MY SKIN

July 28, 2003 was the date of my retirement. At my request, I lived alone in our guest house the first three weeks of retirement. I was still recovering from a rather serious fall as well as heart failure, and was quite aware of my diminishment and losses. I needed to be by myself.

August 15, 2003. Most of my life has been spent helping others and now the time has come for the reverse, for others to help me, and it isn't fun. I seem to be willing to go the extra mile, but when others try to do that for me I feel badly. I don't want help except where I really need it and some things are difficult for me to ask for or accept. For example, the kitchen floor here needs a cleaning and mopping but I can't do that and can't think who to ask to do it for me. My bed is still a problem, as I can't pull, and it needs changing. I am ashamed of these simple needs. Everyone else is so busy that they don't have the extra time so I don't want to ask. I have asked to be alone here so others are respecting my wishes by not dropping by, and this complicates my ability to get help. Can't have it both ways! I need to be more open to what my limitations really are and then ask for the help I need, as others cannot know unless I am willing to tell them. It's as if I don't want others to wash my feet. They too want to be of service to me if I will accept it. That's what community is all about.

August 2005. God caught me a bit late it seems. My stop at Duncan in late June, 2002, came after the purchase of Bethlehem, and the taking on of the responsibilities of ownership. I was not able to go on, knew it in my head and heart, but as my story tells you, and me, it has taken three years of spiritual wandering and direction before God fully got the upper hand. I have now been retired for three years, and life is now closer to the One who truly loves me, my Creator and Redeemer.

DESERT

Called to the desert to seek,
search, learn who I am
the struggle for life in the barren sand
matches my own nothingness
Lost, desolate, my sight occluded

Stillness where winds will not distract, vastness
emptiness that can absorb my own
Day heat, night cold, break the rhythm of my
    depleted mind

Life simple here
miles and miles to wander alone
kick over a stone
look beyond
feel the sun's warmth, presence of God

Parched ground a struggle for life
open, available to desert, death, lifeless
I seek presence, gentle, unique, powerful

Insights quietly come   nourish
too long I have absorbed through open pores, not
    roots
I must go deep, deep into my center
the starkness, barrenness, mold for my rebirth

I walk the desert, tarry there, time, space, solitude
God's light bathes me
stillness of the desert sun's rays
slowly, pacing, the endless distance
depth and breadth.

Solitary, alone in time and space
quiet, stillness I begin to feel my call
Alone   experiencing
My truth   who I am   can be expressed

In stillness, integration
forming and molding my person
I embrace my call with open hands   heart
Becoming at home in my skin.

When I retired in July I stayed nearly a month at our guest house to soak up the peace and quiet and to process the transition and the emotions as they came. Then back to my own room in the monastery.

Vacations are special times; at least they were for me. Over the last thirty-five years they have usually involved travel, often to unexplored areas. This year, not having recovered fully from the heart failure and the result of a fall, I had to stay quite near home. I still wanted to get away and so Eileen came up and we went to Parksville, just a few miles north, where the beaches are quite free of rocks and I can walk on them. After a long afternoon of searching we found a space which, among other amenities, had a fireplace and a very nice kitchen. We booked in. We decided to spend our mornings in silence and prayer, making it a sort of retreat. I was ripe for it. My retreat notes for the next ten days reveal new movements of integration in my being, both body and soul.

September 13, 2003. Yesterday was the first time without severe pain from a recent fall and back injury. Today my energy returned for the first time since April. A dramatic return, just amazing, the difference. I was also high about insights coming up as I tried to relax.

God's presence in my life is nurturing deep within. Just today and yesterday, the return of energy, after I had accepted it was gone, is such an insight into the power and gifts God is always giving me. I had a long time of quiet and prayer with these powerful gifts. I'm more congruent than at any time in my life; I am beginning to deeply acknowledge my shadow, let it be touched by the light of new insight, be expressed and shown as a real part of me. I am becoming more whole, more real and give a more honest representation of myself to others. I need to know which of my life's experiences are mine, those which resonate with my total being as compared to those which were only incidental to my life and represented just the ordinary events of daily living. Strange, it has taken me eighty years to realize a bit about who I am, my unique self, but most important to know how much I am loved and cherished by God. Always have been God loved, and will be, so that I can love me enough to share myself, truly, with any other. Know and honour my past so I can really live my future.

September 16, 2003. Been here nearly a week, working on insights and reading, resting and enjoying. In re-reading some earlier notes I realize now that the last three years have been unusual and dramatic. They were full of tremendous loss, hard work, tension, and yet with tremendous life-giving gain, particularly these last fifteen months.

In May, 1999, I had a pacemaker put in, a new beat to my heart, which stabilized it. I had both knees replaced in July, and for the first time in many years, could live without terrible pain and limitation of mobility. These freedoms were given to me so that I could take on more, and it really came, gushing, flooding overwhelming torrents of disasters large and small, and old as I was I tackled them; I knew no other pattern. Put a challenge before me, and away I would go. The toll was too much, though I couldn't acknowledge it. I did it, and nearly broke. One day in late June, 2002, I caught up with myself, which led me to the Poor Clares.

September 16th, later in day. My life was so full, so full of opposites, good/bad, joy/sorrow, and death/life, that it wasn't full at all. Searching for freedom has been a major thread throughout my entire life; freedom from restrictions, to explore, to reflect, to gain knowledge, to know without knowing why I know, to be who I am. Freedom, like love, begets more. Passed on, it is never still nor limited in any way until I put my own boundaries on it, use it wisely to gain more, become really me, and know it.

Negative thinking, when did it start? Whenever, it grew and grew but the bubble begins to break now I am eighty; I don't need it as a shelter or a place to hide. I don't need to be ashamed, or in any way apologize; I can't do more. I have always really done all I could, but there are limits and I had strange ideas of what they were or should be, compared to reality. It seems this is one of my present callings, to know who I am and know it enough and honour it so that I can share it with others so they, too, may walk the journey of becoming free. I need to look at the patterns of my life: school, army, marriage, college, teaching, leave-taking and all that has come since. These patterns gave direction in my life. This time, here and now, has the possibility of being the very best time of my life, if I will let it be. There is a great drawing to and a great sense of freedom given to me. I am doing less and starting to be, and I can feel the difference.

God has showered me with love and with the openness of mind and heart to go on a new path, no restrictions unless I put them there. I have excellent guides, particularly one who understands my groping and supports me as I make the switch. A great inner strength as gift, presence in a new way. Living rather than dying because I choose life, my own over the death of too-muchness and pushing myself or steeling myself. I can and will say "yes" to these changes.

I notice the ups and downs of spirituality and its growth in my life. Intense digging into, being open to, but not yet ready nor able to go on my own to where I was being called. Now there is time for me, with essentially no obligations, or at least only limited ones. Days free to be, to grow, to create anew.

September 17th. This insightful day started with prayer. Then I started to read *Enduring Grace*, read the preface and on the way a quote from Theresa of Avila. (*Interior Castle* 1.1.2) and the words that just leaped off the page were, "didn't know".

Wouldn't it show great ignorance, my daughters, if some-one, when asked who he was, didn't know, and didn't know his father or mother or from what country he came? Well now, if this would be so extremely stupid, we are incomparably more so when we do not strive to know who we are, but limit ourselves to considering only roughly these bodies. Because we have heard and because faith tells us so, we know we have souls. But we seldom consider the precious things that can be found in this soul, or who dwells within it, or its high value.

I sought my director when I was down, unsure, feeling lost and unsafe. Nebulous feelings, but of such power that I had to stop! Now a new depth, new hearing of call, a new listening, and awareness from another angle if you will, has been a tremendous gift to me. My director's skill, maturity, and spiritual depth has given me a different way to look at my problems, especially to catch me up on who I really am and how God is calling me, spiritually. I had reached a point where I could share the spiritual and I began to feel differently about my strengths and weaknesses. I could love myself because of a new look at how God loves me; actually, not new at all, but I became aware in a different way, which was vitally important to making growth changes. My director stressed that I need to listen to God's love and its outpouring. God will do the healing if and when and as I let go. I must be quiet enough to begin to honour all the quiet nudges that come. I am retired and it's okay to spend lots of time alone in quiet and in prayer. This is my job now.

September 20th. As a child I never bonded and my little body experienced too much separateness and freedom as I was carried about on a pillow. Reflecting back, I see myself as a restless baby and child; that pattern is so deeply ingrained in me. It is still hard for me to contain myself, my quickness, my moving inside myself, in my mind, in my awareness of all about me.

I see myself running as a natural way of getting someplace, or of getting away from hurt or pain. Since earliest childhood I did not like to be held, held back, or in any way restricted. I roamed about the ranch far more than anyone knew. I might have been afraid, but the compulsion to go or to get away was so great, it surmounted any fear.

Today, and in recent months, I can see that I run as a very different expression of my freedom. There have been very few people with whom I've felt safe in my life, and even they don't know why I run because I couldn't put words to it. I am beginning to run to a new-found joy, a freedom of being able to express myself truly, honestly and openly. In other words, run to be safe, to have my needs met, to be close, to experience and feel a place of safety for myself. In some ways I was overwhelmed with need for a safe place, but could never say what my need was. A sense of belonging, which I have never had.

Long ago I knew I could be that safe place for others, that strong person who could be trusted to be there for them; often this was asked of me, with or without words. These past fifteen months have contained times of growth and freedom with a deeper, ever deeper understanding in my heart and soul of the love God gives me, its healing presence within me, if I will let go and let it happen. I am being set free to acknowledge my being a beloved daughter. I acknowledge that being myself, as I am, and meeting my needs, is the prime call for now and into the future. It's like I had to suffer, to give, to do until near death for me to realize my weakness of needing to be needed, so my life would have meaning and any worth at all. Crazy.

There is nothing new here, but on my own, no doubt as a result of life experiences, I could not change my attitudes and behaviours toward myself. When my energy returned eight days ago, and stayed, I discovered the freedom to be a new Jill. I am thankful and grateful beyond anything I had dreamed possible.

September 20th. Without even knowing it, I have been finding God. I have learned to trust people, who can help, and to trust and know that I am a loved daughter. One of my weaknesses is that I don't know how to express what is going on within me. The quiet I have experienced, away from all interruptions, has allowed new listening, a wordless time. I could and did share with my director and am becoming free to accept being loved just because I was created. Separate from the "doing" me. *"You did not choose me, I chose you to go and bear fruit."*

Joy, warmth and quietness have replaced my intensity or need to understand. I just am... and bumps, warts, grey hairs and unfinished business, weaknesses and strengths... anything that makes Jill Jill is not only okay but exactly pleasing to God. I'm aware of more wordless presence, a longing for quiet and peace... wanting to fire up a new understanding and love of myself. There is something new to give, to share, and it's happening as a gift. Big stuff.

September 20th, 8:00 PM. My journey has only now begun; where will it go? I have no idea, but know, deep within, that a listening, peaceful heart, paying attention to God's inner voice to me alone, is what I need. I need verification that what I am hearing and experiencing is a new awareness of how deeply I am loved; in some way, one with God, so that the real letting go can happen and fill me. It's an aloneness, a loneliness that isn't that, but a bursting, all-encompassing passion to be loved.

September 21st, Noon. I'm thinking of all God has gifted to me. It's something I've always intuited or known in my head. It's something I have only occasionally known through my life...at times of intense distress and need, like the surgery at sixteen, and the promise I made then. The knowing that to leave Hank was an okay thing to do. How hard that was. Such great guilt for me, and really painful for Hank. Over the years to feel, deep within, that it was okay and the only way I have known this is to come full circle to some of the revelations of these past ten days. Perhaps I made up for that guilt by doing even more for others. Even more intensity to do good, so that I could be forgiven. Like a penance, over and over. I'm beginning to realize in my heart that even if my motives weren't totally pure or were totally wrong, they were the best I knew, and I did get a lot of counselling. God's loving compassion is a gift to me and forgives me for all those interactions before I even ask.

God is saying, and I'm feeling right now, *"Enough Jill, I love you. I have always understood you did your best. There is no need to beat yourself nor reject my love. I want you closer to me and I've been trying to show you that for a very long time. Open your eyes, ears, mind and heart...let me heal you. You need to accept this healing and embrace it fully so you can receive the fullness of my love for you. I am with you in the direction...the content...the path of your life...even the small mundane events. You know, in your head, my support in these times of change; you are beginning to know it in your heart. Put your heart and mind at ease. Enjoy the gift of quiet I am giving you. I am here in your heart, waiting as you open the door a bit more."*

My quiet response was a conversation.

This is a tremendous gift, Lord, and I accept. Somehow, with the help of trusted friends, I am and will be able to open the door of my heart more fully. I "heart know" that your gifts have always been there, deep, and I acknowledge touching in to them over the years. I need you to continue drawing me deeply, down and in, as the way there. The experience is so tiny but it is there, mine alone.

I can't describe even to You what I am feeling, the gratitude, the compassion and love, but then I don't need to, do I? You already know, and those who have been helping me know too. Continue to give me the way to be quiet with you. To know you will sustain me and fill me continuously with a love I know is your gift.

Somehow I do not have the language for expressing what I am feeling. I don't need it...it's not shareable except by a sense of rightness, strength, and peace. Thank you.

September 21st, Sunday afternoon. I've learned that all I am is gift, and am quite generous in giving to others, time, self, whatever I have. Perhaps I don't keep something long enough to savour it. I know it will be replaced and I won't feel depleted. But I miss the savouring, the taking time with all that is given to me. I'm so sure of more that I pass any gift on easily and think I am doing my part. I'm not, because sometimes the flow of love is so continuous and the path so smooth that I don't take time to savour it. So I am bathed, but not fed, by God's love and concern for me. My compulsion to help others has superseded my own needs. I am beginning to let go and realize God gives to all others, as to me. There is no call to be so quick to give my goodies. Let them stay and grow, slow down the pace. Realize the immensity of each gift and the nuances that are only for me and must stay with me until their action within me can bring about change. I need TIME and quiet to be there and to be with the love and gifts so abundantly all around, to talk, share, and more deeply know the Giver.

September 22nd. Yesterday, in my reading and prayer, the word "shadow" came up. I just noticed it and let it be. Last night and this morning, again, the word! As I got quiet and reminisced about it, I remembered the R. L. Stevenson poem, "My Shadow". I couldn't remember all of it, but as I said it out loud it began to come back. One of my very favourite books as a child was a great big picture book, *A Child's Garden of Verses*, which contained this poem. It is the only one I really liked or remembered.

Like all children, my shadow intrigued me. I tried to control it (so what else is new, Jill), to make it do as I wanted. I learned that it only sometimes was under my control. I remember one day, out at the side of the garage, playing with my shadow. I was very observant and played with it by going in and out of the shade. Sometimes my body was fully in the sun, other times by the shadow of the garage. I also recall noticing what happened when the sun was at different heights. My shadow followed my bodily movements but not my head direction, nor the instructions I gave it. It's like it was a permanent part of me. But I played long and hard with it over a number of years, because in a sense it made me see myself, at least exteriorly. Now, at least seventy or more years since I played with it, I return to its sticking to me, showing a part of me. Now my whole relation to shadow has changed. It is no longer my exterior that I need to explore and accept. The shadow today is the one inside of me... the inside of me I don't reveal to others or even to myself.

Perhaps inadvertently, without my own knowledge and with no intentional disclosure on my part, my shadow is well known and felt by some people very close to me. Unlike my child's play with shadow, today's awareness and understanding of my shadow is hard work. Hard to acknowledge it's there, harder still to take a peek or to begin to work with it, harder still and near impossible to accept this as part of myself. Sometimes it's hard to concede it even exists, let alone to work with it, own it and love it so it can change. My shadow is big; it's everywhere. As I have been reflecting on my feelings and behaviours often involuntarily expressed, I recognize the impact of my shadow on myself and others.

It's a deep responsibility to really own my shadow, to ferret out all the threads and the blind spots left by the years. There are some areas of my shadow that no light has touched, just there, molding away. Yes, I have allowed some light in; have owned some of my shadow over the years. I've had lots of help, but the pattern of my early life just increased the shadow because I knew no other way to survive. That it goes in and out with me wasn't true for me, at least as the dark side of myself was concerned. It just laid there, layer upon layer, not under my active control. It would occasionally get so heavy and black in some area that it would pop out or up, much to my embarrassment, and be another source of putting myself and it down. I wasn't ready to work with more than the edges.

In some sense, the understanding comes to me through the words of my director; "God will do the healing". And now I know God will. I expect what has happened is that by letting love into that area of my being, inviting God there, being aware right now of the warmth and sense of presence in a new way, God's presence has already begun to effect change in my shadow. I'm willing, eager, and wanting and waiting for God's work in my shadow to point out to me the next steps in my growth and conversion. I know God will do this because I am now begging and asking that God be in my awareness in a new way.

I still want my shadow to be a part of me and like it or not, it always will be, but the inside shadow is less fearful and I am accepting it as a part of myself in a new way. It is the spot of God's presence working in me and perhaps the greatest gift ever.

"*Goes in and out with me and what can be the use of him is more than I can see.*" Stevenson's words may be true for him, but not for me. I need to see deep into the shadow and accept it, as I somehow feel that God is most present in my shadow and has very important truths to share with me about it. My shadow dances for joy, for recognition, and wants to be a real part of me. I don't want to control it, just to embrace it, and God with it.

Tuesday, 23rd. Neediness. Speaking need is only the first step. It must be filled, I know now, only by God. In fact, all the answer is inside me and always was, is, and will be. Intensity, insights, and understanding are the tips of God's greatest gifts, to be invited in to warm me, to seek out the empty spaces, to fill the spaces for years left blank and empty. To make me more me, and more God-filled, so that I am totally one with Him, then I can die. Intensity, insights, understandings are all part and parcel of the same thing. All are gifts of God. All bring heightened awareness and abilities beyond my control, they allow me to do more, to understand more, and offer me new directions to follow.

There is a sense of newness in insights, understandings, and intensity. Intensity at first did not seem to fit here, but it does. Intensity is my way of expressing the compulsion, the drive, the zest to experience all of life. I don't want to miss anything and this includes doing—to experience, to give, to share, to be free, to make choices, really in all aspects of life I want 100% participation. Perhaps it is the quiet after the storm, or as I have often said, do it all and quickly, so that the next bit of time is mine to do with as I wish. The time of quiet is my creative time or time to fritter away, or time to fill up, and time to waste, as well. In my long life, all the above have been true. Sometimes all at once. Now I know a longing for and a striving to be filled. It's what I speak of as neediness...a hollow empty space. It will be filled when I will let myself speak it out, but unfortunately my need is often so great I can't express it. Scared by it? I'm afraid I may turn others off. Even speaking of it to others might be disastrous.

September 23rd. Filled with Love. The being filled with love is a mystery, and yet not. I realize, as it came to me a day or so ago, that the fullness of God's love within me is total. I am totally full and there is no room for more. Filled up...yet not. It's like a stream, flow of love coming into and through the tissues and veins of my body. If these passages are smooth I really receive the love, but it doesn't nurture deeply. I am filled to overflowing already so there is no place for tarrying or staying awhile. There needs to be some roughness or something to slow the passage of love. The love pours in and goes out to others. But I need to learn how to slow it, so as to savour it, to really, deeply let God's love into all my being, into each cell of my being.

I need to let God touch me differently. Not only a head awareness of God, but to realize that God wants to be with me totally, so that healing love can take place. I need to open all my pathways, to receive, to allow myself to be bathed with God's love. God's particular love for me comes to me, but I know I've not let it be with me, or let it burn a special mark into any areas of my life. My experiences, my knowledge, my sharing, my gifting to others is all very fine, but I have not thought of myself as worthy of God's being so uniquely with me. Rather, I have accepted this love largely at the head level, and only a bit at the heart level. Recently I have become aware that this is only a fragment of the unique, intimate love God has for me.

It's like God is longing for me to wake up, to live because of this love. To fully receive it, or to realize that the gift of love, of life, is beyond my wildest dreams... my explosion with love has not yet come. I really don't know how to let all this become, so I am asking for the gift of this deeper intimacy and you, God, will give it to me, I am sure.

There is much in my life—carelessness, thought-lessness, sin, ego, poor judgment, denial of truth, lazi-ness—which needs to be acknowledged and put out for a healing love bath, so it can be let go. God, this morning I ask for your help in all these areas. My un-bounded gratitude for the awareness you give, and have given to me. I love You and begin to feel a drawing to an openness to You in a deeper, more fulfilling way. This is my prayer.

This retreat set a new and heightened awareness of where I was, in relation to my God. I heard and an-swered the call to continue to work with my director, and as my story has told you, these next years were dif-ficult, some horrendously hard, but with the new sup-port of my God I felt growing in me, they passed rather quickly. I thank God that I could hear the continual call to a full and healed life.

Light Dawns

April 23, 2005. About 7:30 this evening, I decided I wanted to track down where I was two years ago, at the time when I went into heart failure and ultimately had to quit working at Bethlehem. I found the spot in my journal and at first thought I had not written much. But was I ever wrong. The last couple of days I have realized how very differently I am handling oodles of things, particularly some relationships with friends, but also myself. A friend and I have gotten into it a couple of times just recently, and in the process of owning up to our faults and asking pardon we did some valuable work. I realize how much I have changed. Life is often painful and these few episodes have helped me to re-remember relationships with other people in my life, especially family. It has been very valuable and enlightening. I went to bed early and after a bit of reading, went to sleep, only to wake in an hour. I was most uncomfortable with my neuropathy and then immediately my mind was busy with the kinds of things I had been into just before I went to sleep. I just let myself go with what came up, grabbed my cross and held it and fingered it and realized again the blessings the cross has brought me. I did not ask Jesus to stop the process or in any way change it as it was obviously important.

Reviewing the journal notes told me that indeed I was very seriously ill a couple of years ago, the heart failure was not in check. I wanted to retire in April, but the community asked me to stay through August, though I said at that time I didn't know if I could make it. It was a terrible time, deciding I needed to stay on at BRC until after we had the meeting with a facilitator in late August. What a hell. I could and did tell my director how I was feeling and she in no way minced words in telling me what I needed to do. Even though she was correct, I could not bring myself to make my needs honestly known to the community, though I did try in some ways. I now think I was just not believable. Without my realizing it fully, I put on a mask of making light of my true feelings, energy level, and personal fear about the heart problem, and I did not accurately portray what I was doing to myself.

So, as usual, on the surface I looked more or less okay, tired, older perhaps, but still going nearly full steam ahead, or at least that is what some people saw, or needed to see. I put them in that frame of mind by saying one thing and doing another. My actions belittled the harsh truth. A pattern all my life. I had a need to put forth a good front, false though it may be, and if it was to my detriment, I had learned to stuff it and apparently not care. This was my way of living out my survivor stance and a darned poor one, I might add.

It is apparent to me that some do not really hear me when I say I can't take it, even if others need me to be available. I try to respect others' needs. My questions: What about my needs? Am I selfish to say I can't handle it? What is my responsibility? The question came up for me, "What would Jesus do?"

I am amazed as I read my notes what a struggle it has been for me to honestly look at my whole life and all the good and all the ugly stuff and all the ways, good and bad, that I handled things that came my way. It has been a significant journey, at a rather slow, steady pace, and now perhaps an end is in sight.

Several strong words come to mind. Over the past year or more the word diminishment has come to mean a great deal to me, both positive and negative. The passage from Chardin in *The Divine Milieu* has stuck in my mind and now in my heart.

"*It was a joy to me, O God, in the midst of the struggle, to feel that in developing myself I was increasing the hold that you have upon me; it was a joy to me, too, under the inward thrust of life or amid the favourable play of events, to abandon myself to your providence. Now that I have found the joy of utilizing all forms of growth to make you, or to let you, grow in me, grant that I may willingly consent to this last phase of communion in the course of which I shall possess you by diminishing in you.*"

The essence is that only when my ego diminishes and I let go is there room for Jesus/God to come in. Basically simple, but oh so hard to get deeply ingrained in my heart. Another word is desire, which comes from the book *Franciscan Prayer* that I have recently studied. Finally getting, after many readings and much prayer, what that really means. God's desire for me... followed by my desire for God.

Another strong word is gaze...and the picking up of the Franciscan cross as a "feelie", which has been very important. Christ's outstretched arms want to have me come and share whatever is going on for me. Share fully and from the sharing, in a very intimate way, receive and experience the total love that is given. Words cannot express the change this has made in me.

Back to the question, "Are you lonely?" I had no idea at all how lonely I was for a loving God. I had a life-long loneliness deeply sensed and only rarely satisfied. I also know that absence/presence will in some ways keep that loneliness differently, as it has now become a longing for God.

Certainly one of the greatest gifts I have received, over and over again these past three years, has been the invitation by my director to say anything I needed to say, sensible, crazy, and in whatever manner. I felt free to say it all out and never stopped from doing so. Whatever I said she accepted. A gift of God. I have done some deep soul searching and truth telling. It was not easy but I did it and I am so grateful for that. A special gift of my director is that she accepts me and this has allowed me to open up. Even if I can't do what I say I will try, I can still return and won't feel too ashamed of my failure.

At all times she modeled Christ's love. Challenged, I began and have taken a few steps on the road to knowing how loveable I am. This has helped me be able to stand there in some of the hard spots of my everyday life. How do I know this? Well it is evident in my prayer. I have found, for some time now, great changes in prayer. I have found that I indeed need, at least at this time, and probably always, lots of time by myself. I just never got it before. Being instead of doing has been the clue. I am finding that with the quieter day, the total loss of intensity for some months, I pick up an idea or thought from some reading, or something I have been mulling over, and letting myself slip into my chair, can go deeply to prayer, to a new sense of listening with my heart. Not needing words, but just being there. I honestly think this change in the last few months has been most important and one that certainly wouldn't have happened if I had not already begun to quiet down.

There is another thing, and that is how my readings over the past two years have all tended to set me up for this deeper, more intimate relationship with Jesus. On vacation in Parksville with Sister Eileen, I renewed my friendship with Chardin, Julian, and St. Clare, among others. One of the best realizations about all that has been going on for me these last five years, particularly the last three, is that I was not readily available for change. I realize I lived my life on an intense level, and the ups and downs, struggles, and hurts were just part of the moment, now accepted as such. The door opened on a new life, for new it is. The time now is just different, and I have changed sufficiently to realize how God has worked through all these years to call me closer and closer, and to understand what God always desired in our relationship. This is a great gift that I can hardly begin to understand deeply, though I know it is true.

If I had known all this years ago, then perhaps I would have been a more useful person, a better child, mother, wife, teacher, sister, but I was not yet ready. Given my gifts and my struggles, my fears and my tainted emotions, I have always tried to do my best. So... I am grateful for the road to Duncan and there is much more to understand about how to share the gifts given to me. I have said little about my relationship with Sister Eileen here, which has been so important each of these last thirty-three years. Both of us have grown immeasurably in these past years. We have shared much of our journal work with each other, have gone to Father Henry together for spiritual guidance, and I have shared my own work, here in Canada. I look forward to again having time with her and will cherish the deep, honest sharing we always find possible. Interesting that as I sit here at the keyboard and my fingers and thoughts are working openly and well, I still can't even begin to express both the gratitude and awe of these past growing years, but it just can't be put into words, not meant to be said, just felt deep within. Maybe I am beginning to know I am loveable just as I am and am growing to become.

April 25, 2005. I realize the pattern of my life has been so busy and intense that it took a long time to get quiet, to really listen, to make heart changes. The quiet and reflection and slower pace have shown me that it is all about really listening deeply to the specifics of my call and flowing with it gently Today I know, for the first time in my life, that I have said everything I need to say. Light dawns... light has healed in thought, in action, and reaction, and there is still sufficient strong light for the way ahead. No longer am I carrying gaping or bleeding wounds. The scars are there, yes, but as part of the land on which I now stand. The work of tomorrow will not be tangled in the web of the past, but free to bring the fruit to harvest.

LIGHT

I walk in darkness
pulled, bent, misshapen
Light   life   gifts needed
are absorbed   acknowledged

Insights, short bursts of presence
entice me
to the deepest source,
God's light

Prayer, forgiveness   tools for eternal light
In deep despair, darkness, God is most present
the cloak of darkness tossed off
by sincere quest for light

My sight occluded
opacities of my own making
light obscured from me

Light often apparent where it is not
as in the contrast between two darknesses
life here,
sometimes I hide in shadow not able to take God's
        light

Yet, I am a child of light
even in my duality, darkness/light
Light is
the fullness of life/death
when with God all light becomes

EPILOGUE

As I reflect back on becoming a Benedictine over thirty years ago, it is obvious that I didn't know what I was getting into... and in some ways I still don't. Answering whatever I heard in a Call drew me into a completely different way of life. Today, as I was thinking of all these years, the image of a holiday gift basket of fruits came to mind. The basket in my mind's eye had very attractively shaped fruits, round grapefruit, a slim and deeply yellow banana, bunches of grapes, both red and white, a bright orange persimmon, an avocado, and underneath, as a base, apples, oranges and pears. Sprinkled around among the fruits were walnuts, pecans, hazel nuts and almonds. All fruits and nuts gathered together, with a warm chartreuse film and a big bow of the same colour, an immediate invitation to sample it.

In some ways this is an example of my religious life. I could immediately put names to some of the fruits, which would indicate some of our practices. The apples, oranges, and pears would represent the day by day gathering to pray with other members of our community. Some of the more special fruits might signify special events or days. Grapes represent community, with many members all sort of the same, yet not.

The basket was colourful and balanced. Individually the fruits were quite ordinary and yet, in their togetherness, their impact was greater than the sum of the individuals. So it is, as we live in community. Our numbers may be small, but the fact that we live, work, pray and play together makes us bigger than ourselves and able to have a surplus to share with others. Over the years, a blessing for our community is that most of us have been able to live together. While each of us works on growth and transformation individually, the support, often silent, of others on their journey helps us persevere in following our calls. Life-giving, rhythmic changes are evident only with hindsight, and the passage of years. Light, dark, and shadow are evident in all our lives, but thankfully we are not all in the same space at the same time. The light of one helps balance the other when they are in their shadow, or having a dark time.

Here in Nanaimo, we are still a small family; we gather at one table daily, pray together, share special events that come up as we live our lives. It's not easy to live so closely with others; like a family, we know each other too well, can't hide much. Just thinking about living in a home with a number of adult women, all very high-profile, successful women, makes me realize the large measure of graces we receive from God.

Group decision-making or at least a sounding out of consensus, helps set up the parameters for community living. Each of us has to put up with the growing edge of all our sisters; always a challenge. We find our own niche and way through life, sometimes limping along, perhaps lonely, yet other times find willing hands or words to help us. One of our goals is to make changes in our life patterns that will make living life a bit easier for each other. Not an easy task...but neither is the single life, or the married life. I have tried them all and my summation is that community life, hard as it has been at times, is completely right for me, both the community I am in and the place I call home. I have never been happier. I really enjoy retirement, though I am not sure it is quite as self-directed or as full of free time as I thought it would be. I know I have been much more capable of helping and serving God's people than if I had continued to do an independent ministry. I am glad for the community support and now that I am old and retired, know that they will continue to meet my needs. I do not stay because I have to, and no one could live the life of a religious except in response to a continuous call to the life. Just recently, I was a participant in a workshop which asked us to look at our initial wounds. I have been aware of the lack of bonding with my mother all my life; it just didn't happen. Fortunately, I took some reflective time before I answered, because, as I have been working on this book, I realize that my wound came elsewhere.

My wound was not knowing a loving God. As I said earlier, my first idea of God, from about age five, was that God was a record keeper with a full and detailed list of all my bads; "God doesn't like bad girls" was the message that came across in word and action. I did not know about forgiveness then, and did not catch on to God's forgiveness and love for several eons of time.

I have also had, from my earliest wanderings on the ranch, a sense of wonder about nature. The life cycles, the order, the uniqueness of each blade of grass or flower, the seasons, and the living/dying, drew me to be deeply interested in the how and why of all before me. So many unanswered questions, as I tried to comprehend the order and disorder in nature. None of the responses ever put me in touch with a Creator. I have often said that I am a risk taker, perhaps also a runner. I have tackled many, many problems, come up against brick walls and had to make sudden turns. I have allowed myself to hear a new call and gone on to seek new direction. Is this another gift of God, courage? Courage, yes, because I stood there or stood up to very difficult and abrupt life changes and diminishments. I went forward, somehow knowing that a way would come, a new path or perhaps a new companion for my journey. The truth is, I had many changes, experiences and yes, skins, but all led to fullness and a hope-filled life.

December 21, 2005. Old age embraced. Yesterday I could express for the first time what has been new in my life. It seems as if an eighty-two year old finding something new is likely to be suspect.

It was, at first, for me. However, I kept at it and now realize there is lots of newness going on.

I was aware some months ago, back in April, that I had said everything I needed to say. By that I meant that I have kept nothing back from my director, who helped me sort it out. There was nothing hidden, no agenda not brought up because of shame, fear, or lack of responsibility. I was aware of a great sense of freedom because of the deliberate talking out of things as they came up. Now, I am at a new crossroads, and speaking it out fully yesterday made a lot of sense to me and continues to bring awe and wonder to my heart and eyes and mind.

My work, in the sense that there are assigned tasks, new goals, and responsibilities, is now finished. I resigned recently from the last responsibility, because it was timely and also right for me, at my stage of diminishment. It was a good feeling, one I could never have anticipated, no matter how much I might have thought of the future.

I am, in a sense, free to do as I wish, which quickly brings to mind that the freedom thus found brings the unvoiced responsibility to use it wisely and for others. It is one of the gifts of God, so that I can be useful to others. This is abundantly clear to me. The responsibility comes not only in having to do my job well, but from my desire to meet others' needs; not the same level.

It's like loving. Giving and receiving love and always having enough to give totally, and knowing for sure more will come, with the feeling that it is already here; it's not possible to ever be empty. Such a gift!

I am overwhelmed with gratitude for these understandings of God's love for me, which are coming more clearly to my heart. There is a need to acknowledge again that all these understandings are gifts, are transforming, and show God's love for me.

I look back to see where the gifts came from and the image that comes to me is of a prickly artichoke, taken apart leaf by leaf, each slowly scraped off by the teeth, enjoying the bite, then taking another leaf and eventually reaching the heart of the choke. There one finds a hairy barrier which, when scooped out, leaves a small empty cup at the heart which holds several mouthfuls that seem more than enough for the journey ahead. If a special presentation is desired you can just rip off the leaves, scoop out the center, and fill it with salad or sauce.

This image speaks to me of the years of handling prickly bits, hurts if you will, then realizing that when I reached the center and cleaned it properly there was space for God to put a special gift, and He/She has done so over and over again.

My life, starting from age twenty-nine, has been one of searching for this Creator God and what was in His/Her mind for me. So many paths, but never getting the point. Or perhaps the point wasn't sharp enough in my mind to penetrate to my heart, staying safely in my head. I kept up the search for God's love throughout these many years. Somehow I did go on. No easy answers, many dead ends, many times of confusion and bewilderment. The richness of a more responsive and easy communion with a loving God has been the prime result of these last five years of struggle. I am grateful to all those who have helped me on my way. I was lonely and longing. I realize that this book has been an opening, healing process. Reflecting back, and reading my journals and their place in my story, makes me realize how I have changed, matured and become even freer as the book has been written.

I wrote a first draft for my family and included no journals whatsoever. When I first saw my director in June, 2002, I began to share with her bits from my journal, but not exactly as I wrote it. Gradually, I could be more open. As I started to write this more full life story I included some reflections but did not actually include much material from the journals. Progressively, I found myself not censoring my deepest thoughts, and sometimes I shared directly and fully from my journals. Ultimately, of course, I realized that some of the material they contained, which had helped me to heal, could help others. In re-reading and realizing the depth of this journey, I risk sharing my struggle and the unfolding of God's love in me, hoping it may be helpful.

In April, 2005, I realized I had told it all. Mostly, though, I have had good, deep talks with my God… and am overwhelmed by the love I feel…the touches of presence, coming and going; and knowing that, as Julian of Norwich said, all shall be well. How do I know? Well, my gracious God has given me the tools to work with, and they work. I can identify some of them; they are simple: awareness, silence, quiet, and a willingness to share and trust others.

Today, if asked the question, "Are you lonely?" My answer would be no. I know God's love in a wholly, holy, different way and now the loneliness is a longing which can and is being filled. Presence. I really hear and can acknowledge call.

I wrote these words in 1983 for my book *Lectio*. I read them now again, reflect on them. A world of difference is apparent to me. I am not the same woman; these words were head written; now they speak from my heart.

Being there...   dwelling there with God
Enlightenment... surprises...   let in the new
Presence found in aloneness   simplicity...
a vastness   emptiness to be filled
Listening...   then a yes to God
With fidelity...   constancy
Enveloped in presence,
Finding my own true self
God's light...   the Son's warmth
In quiet, stillness...   a creative tension
A seed planted...   growth to wholeness
Integrating the encounters
Awed by touch

So, you see, I entered religious life and God has sustained me all these years; God, who is now so present in my heart that it is nearly breaking with joy at this new relationship. An eighty-three-year-old woman who is filled to the brim with life, and can't wait for what next is to come. God is ever so good.

STEPS

Steps go to the depths
of forest   or sea
to the hidden places
the unknown

Suddenly
stepping stones of my past

Not buried
laid down to lead

The way to new life
a step at a time

✠

ACKNOWLEDGEMENTS

Who helps another write a book? There are several possible answers, if one is thinking of an autobiography. Thankfully I have had many excellent assistants; those who lived part of my journey with me and could verify a particular event, some who read drafts and encouraged me to add more detail, and others who wanted more spiritual journal material included. So my thanks to Bonnie Loehr, Eileen Garcia, Elli Boray, Roger Kimmerley, Sister Pat Brady and Sister Eileen Kraemer who shared insights with me as I went along, and made it possible for me to take the time to write my story. Pam Van Reis has offered her sharp eye and fine mind and encouraged me to say more, cut in some places, and has helped me in sorting out the masses of material found in my heart and head.

The editing, typesetting, layout and cover were done by Hiro Boga who, when I first met her, got in tune quickly with the work I was trying to do. Her meticulous attention to detail and her years of experience as a writer and editor have put the final touches to my work. There are many others, far too many to name, who have supported my efforts and I thank them.

AUTHOR'S NOTE

Even to this day, I continue to be a stranger to myself. My story includes a struggle to have a deep relationship with God, and it has taken my entire life to come to grips with God's unique call to me. Twenty-seven years in a marriage, three years listening to "what's next" and now thirty-five years as a Benedictine Sister have kept challenges ever before my eyes and heart. The last twenty-four years here in Nanaimo, B.C. bring an awareness of the fullness of every minute of my long life. Since my retirement at age eighty I have continued to be full of energy and have time to write, take pictures, cook a bit and of course continue to pray and get ready to meet my God. Life has been full to overflowing, and there is still no sign of a let up.

ALSO BY SISTER JILL AIGNER

✠

Seek Abide: Scripture Themes
with Reflective Questions

His Way My Way: A Growth Journal
(Inclusive language)

Foundations Last Forever: Lectio Divina. A mode of
Scripture Prayer

✠

To order please contact:
Monastery Press
2329 Arbot Rd
Nanaimo, BC
V9R 6S8 Canada
Tel: 250-741-1704
monasterypress@shaw.ca
www.houseofbreadmonastery.com

Retail price: CAN$19.95; US$18.95; plus shipping.
Bulk order discounts available for book retailers.